What They'ı
about *The Allurir*

"Faithful. Engaged. Direct. Belief declines, but our relationship with God need not dissolve. Carrell Jamilano offers a practical, honest, return-to-God call that meets young adult readers and their parents where they are. She recognizes the struggles of faith because she has experienced them herself. These range from actively questioning God's presence to routine boredom and distractions. Jamilano reminds us God seeks relationship with us in all places, usual and unusual alike. She offers practical advice to start and maintain a prayer life that alerts readers to God's abundant and sustaining love."

Jeffrey Marlett, PhD
College of Saint Rose

"Carrell Jamilano brings a true evangelist's gift for storytelling to this refreshing book on the spiritual life. With great vulnerability and compassion for the real-life struggles of young people, *The Alluring Voice of God* is a precious resource for individual or group use. Invitingly clear and simple in its presentation, it is packed with authentic teaching and powerful questions that will ignite a deeper conversation with God in all who read it."

Lisa Mladinich
Author and founder of WonderfullyMade139.com

"I wish this book had been available when I was a young Catholic! Knowing that experience is the basis of all theology that is worth the name, Carrell Jamilano has woven together seamlessly her education and her personal experience as both inquirer and director to create this guidebook for young people seeking an experiential basis for their faith. She presents traditional, time-honored practices, such as the five types of prayer and the rosary, as liberating rather than constraining, showing readers how they can creatively use those methods to create a distinctive path filled with the joy and love of a deeply faith-filled life. With eminently practical tips and insightful reflection questions, Carrell offers direction to help her readers truly "find God in all things." Although it is written especially for young adult Catholics and teens, all people who want to deepen and revitalize their relationship with God will richly benefit from finding a place for this book on their bookshelf and in their heart."

Pamela Hedrick, PhD
St. Joseph's College of Maine

The Alluring Voice of God

FORMING DAILY ENCOUNTERS

Carrell Jamilano

Liguori

Imprimi Potest: Stephen T. Rehrauer, CSsR, Provincial
Denver Province, the Redemptorists

Published by Liguori Publications, Liguori, Missouri 63057

Liguori Publications, a nonprofit corporation, is an apostolate of the
Redemptorists (Redemptorists.com).

Phone: 800-325-9521 *Web:* Liguori.org

The Alluring Voice of God: Forming Daily Encounters
Copyright © 2021 Carrell Jamilano
ISBN 978-0-7648-2841-6
Library of Congress Control number: 2021912624

25 24 23 22 21 / 5 4 3 2 1

First Edition

Printed in the United States of America

Cover design: Wendy Barnes

....

 About the author: A spiritual director and speaker,
Carrell Jamilano has led youth and young-adult
ministries. She cohosts *WOMAN: Strong Faith, True
Beauty* for the Shalom World television channel and
has appeared on programs produced by the CatholicTV
network. Her writing has been published by *Liguorian* magazine, Life
Teen International, and The Upper Room. Carrell earned her master of
arts in pastoral theology at Saint Joseph's College of Maine, a Catholic
institution. She blogs at CatholicSpiritualDirector.com/blog.

CONTENTS

DEDICATION

First, I dedicate this book to the triune God, Blessed Mother Mary, and our communion of saints for their loving and merciful presence in my life. All of you inspire me to be selfless and holy.

To my husband, AJ, who works tirelessly to promote justice in our world. Your compassionate heart reflects Christ's love to me every day, and I am incredibly blessed to be married to you!

To my daughter, Maryli, whose unconditional love and bountiful exuberance continually remind me of our good Father in heaven. I thank God for you each day and pray you will receive the joy and graces that come from our beloved faith. You have captivated me from the moment you began developing in my womb!

To my parents, Thelma, Hermie, and Filipinas, for always supporting me in every endeavor and encouraging me in my faith. I love all of you so much!

To my youth, young adults, and directees—thank you! You fill my life with great meaning and purpose. I pray this book leads you closer to the One who loves us most!

Introduction

- Sometimes I feel as if God isn't listening to me.

- I want to have a closer relationship with God, but I just don't know where to start.

- My prayer life is incredibly repetitive and dry. I want to pray, but why is it that when others pray, they get a sense of peace? When I pray, I feel so empty.

- I pray, pray, and pray, but I just don't understand what God is calling me to do.

- Does God really speak to people? What does he sound like? How can I tell if he is speaking to me?

These are the questions that reverberate in my mind. They are the questions that—as a spiritual director—my youth, young adults, and directees pose to me as they share their desire to draw closer to God and follow his will. How many nights have I found myself listening and guiding someone who needed help understanding where God is amid their struggles? Their questions, frustrations, and yearnings to hear God respond to their prayers weighed on my thoughts.

My heart went out to them because I also had felt that way. I was a cradle Catholic who went to Sunday Mass and prayed the rosary daily. Still, I had no concept of what a true relationship with God looked like. I didn't know how to have a meaningful relationship with him, how to discern what he was calling me to do, or even how to listen to his voice.

What Do Sacramental Preparation Programs Need?

When I was a director of youth and young-adult ministry, our young-adult group proved to be the most challenging—and the most rewarding. I had been fortunate to see some of my junior high and high school participants become empowered, faith-filled, young-adult parish leaders. But I also witnessed the slow growth and even spiritual decline in some members of our young-adult group. I spent countless hours striving to develop a ministry and retreat geared to their specific needs, and I desperately desired to reach those young adults who would attend Mass but who I would never hear from. What happened to all our newly confirmed teens who were once on fire for God? Why don't we see them anymore after they receive the sacrament of confirmation? Why are there so many young adults missing from our pews? What are they seeking?

According to a Gallup poll, dating from the 1950s there has been an alarming 36 percent decrease in weekly Catholic church attendance. In addition, there has been a significant increase in people with no religious affiliation. "Over the past two decades," Gallup reports, "the percentage of Americans who do not identify with any religion grew from 8 percent in 1998–2000 to 13 percent in 2008–10, and 21 percent" from 2018–20. Although this trend is being seen in all religious groups and all ages in the United States, Gallup says this decrease in religious affiliation is most pronounced among millennials—America's young adults. While many religious worshipers in the United States are aging, those who self-identify as agnostic, atheist, or "nothing in particular" are getting younger.

Sadly, I am not surprised. Like me, numerous Catholics have been catechized through years of sacramental preparation. But once they complete these programs, far too many leave with knowledge about God but little understanding of how to develop a personal, living relationship with him. They can list the Ten Commandments, recite the Apostles' Creed, name the sacraments, and describe several saints, but if you were to ask a majority what their relationship with God is like, they might answer: "Good, I guess," "It could be better," "What do you mean by that? I go to church on Sundays, and I believe in God. I enjoyed the classes," or "Uh...it's OK. I still find prayer rather difficult, but I still like going to church."

If I were to ask these same individuals how they hear God speak to them or how they see God responding to their prayers, most would shrug their shoulders and give me a look of bewilderment. How, then, can we expect our youth and young adults to hold fast to our beloved Catholic faith when many have yet to know God personally?

A Pew Research Center "Religious Landscape Study" reports that the percentage of Catholics who say they believe in God has dropped by 8 percent. Even so, among those who still identify as Catholic, there is a growing interest in daily prayer, prayer groups, and meditation. In comparison to an earlier study, the percentage of Catholics who pray daily, attend weekly prayer groups, and meditate weekly has increased by 1 percent, 4 percent, and 4 percent, respectively. The overall numbers, though alarming, reveal what

Catholics seek the most—a deeper connection to God. They yearn to see his face, hear his voice, and feel his presence in their everyday lives, and when they lack the means to do so, they leave. It is not enough to know facts about God. It is not enough to know popular Scripture passages from the Bible. It is not enough to know what the Catholic faith teaches. Catholics want to encounter God in profound and life-changing ways. Those ways begin with prayer.

Prayer Is a Living, Personal Relationship with God

As a spiritual director, I have the privilege of accompanying directees on their spiritual journey to God. Spiritual direction seeks to deepen the directee's prayer life through the guidance of the Holy Spirit, the ultimate spiritual director. Directees often seek spiritual direction when they need help discerning God's will, guidance on how to overcome obstacles in prayer, clarity on how God may be working in their lives, assistance recognizing God's presence throughout their day, and instruction on how to distinguish God's voice, among other reasons. Like my youth and young adults, directees want to feel God's loving presence and hear him speak in response to their prayers.

What many are missing, however, is a fundamental understanding and experience of what prayer is. It's not just a set of memorized lines or something to check off a to-do list. Prayer is the way we communicate with God and the way in which God communicates with us. It is an ongoing encounter with our Creator, Redeemer, and Friend. As such, prayer requires two essential actions from us: talking to and listening to God.

For many of us, talking to God comes easier than listening. Still, we may try to keep parts of our lives hidden from God or fall into a routine of sharing the same things over and over. Listening to God presents even more challenges. We think: "How can I hear God when he is not physically present?" What is so incredible about God is that he can speak to us not only through human tongues but in everything he created. His voice compels us. His words change us. His presence enlivens us. We cannot help but be moved and inspired when we discover his voice in our lives.

Often, the reason we cannot hear God is because we do not understand how he speaks. Since God is limitless, so are the ways in which he chooses to communicate. God can speak to us in the stillness of our hearts. God can speak to us through Scripture, his living word. God can speak to us through traditions handed down to us by the apostles, the closest friends of Christ. God can speak to us in unexpected ways that are unique to us alone. God's loving presence and compassionate voice is closer to us than we might imagine. The key is uncovering the tools that will help us become more aware of his voice in our lives.

Who Is *The Alluring Voice of God* for?

This book is for all Catholics—especially young adults— who want to develop a meaningful relationship with God. It is for those who have been catechized but lack the tools to communicate and listen to him. It is meant to help seekers understand the various ways God speaks to us and what is needed to foster a fruitful prayer life. Throughout the book, you will find sections I call "Prayer Traps." These sidebars illuminate common obstacles to prayer and tips to overcome them. More specifically, these sections point out and clarify misunderstandings many have about God and our relationship with him.

How to Use This Book

The Alluring Voice of God can be used in two ways: for private reflection and personal growth and within a class or small-group setting.

I recommend you complete "For Practice and Reflection" at the end of each chapter. These activities and questions enable seekers to experience firsthand how God speaks to them. They provide the means to put into practice all that is learned from the chapter. These are the tools that will help you discern God's loving voice in your life.

For church ministers, religion teachers, or those who wish to use this book for a faith-formation class, prayer group, youth or young-adult gathering, or any other small group, please visit CatholicSpiritualDirector.com, where you will find sample lesson plans for each chapter.

May this book help draw you closer to God, and may you be at peace knowing that God hears you and responds to every prayer in your heart!

With joy in Christ,
Carrell Jamilano

CHAPTER 1

God Wants to Hear from You

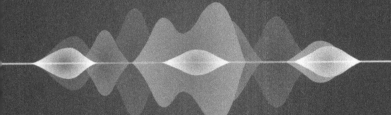

> **"Whether we realize it or not, prayer is the encounter of God's thirst and ours."**
>
> ### ST. AUGUSTINE

his was a first. I had never had a catechist take a group that I was part of outside of the classroom for a lesson. I was used to the same routine: start off in prayer, read through a dull book that didn't relate to me, try to ignore my annoying classmates goofing off behind me, and then go home...uninspired. Today, however, we had no ordinary catechist. He was a friend, but he felt more like an older brother. We both sang and were part of the youth choir, and tonight he was our substitute teacher. I was curious to see how he would teach our class.

As we walked from the classroom to the church, my curiosity grew. *Where are we going?* I thought. *Is he taking us to the church to pray? What will he say? How did he come to so believe in God that he spends his free time being a catechist—or at least subbing for one?* As my thoughts wandered, we stopped at a statue of Christ, who was depicted dying on the cross, that was illuminated by two spotlights.

"Take some time to look at Christ Jesus on the cross," he finally said. "What do you see? What do you feel? What thoughts come to mind when you gaze at this passionate scene?"

I thought to myself, *What do I see? I see sheer anguish, nails violently piercing his hands and feet, blood streaming down his body. Then I see his eyes. They look upward, at peace. What do I feel? Well, I guess I feel confused. His body says one thing, but his eyes say another. I feel disturbed by this horrific death—and afraid because I understand we're all capable of the kind of cruelty inflicted on our Lord. My thoughts? I don't understand why anyone would choose to die like this. I heard that Jesus willingly allowed himself to be whipped, stripped naked, mocked, spit upon, nailed to a cross, and die in seeming disgrace. All for us. How can he love us this much?*

My thoughts were suddenly interrupted. *Knock. Knock. Knock.* I looked up and saw my friend's hand lifted high, knocking on the cross as one would tap on a door. "Do you hear that?" he asked the class. "That is Christ, our God, knocking on your heart. He is always knocking on our hearts. Why? Because he loves us. He wants to be near us, heal us, transform us. He wants to speak to us. He doesn't want to barge in and force us to open our hearts to him. That's not his way. He is a God of peace, healing, and great love. So, he keeps knocking." *Knock. Knock. Knock.* "Will you answer his call? Will you let him enter? Will you open that door to him? Will you allow him to be a part of your life, let him live in your heart? It's your choice."

My friend was so impassioned and, until then, I had yet to meet someone who was truly on fire for God. He seemed to know and love him. That night I left inspired.

Weeks later, I was at the piano reflecting on that class. I started fiddling with the keys until I landed on a sweet, melancholic melody. I felt called to write everything I was feeling—thoughts, doubts, frustrations, and everything in between:

How can I believe in you
if I can't see your face,
if I can't even feel you?
How do I know that you're always right beside me?

Help me to love you.
Help me to see.
Open up my eyes, Lord.
Open up my heart.

As I finished pairing words with melody, I realized I had composed my first song. More significantly, I wrote and sung my very first prayer to God! Matthew 6:7 says, "In praying, do not babble like the pagans, who think that they will be heard because of their many words." My prayer life had been babbling until now. I spewed memorized words without taking the time to really understand them.

That sung prayer was a catalyst that renewed my relationship with God because I meant every word of it. For the first time, I prayed with my whole heart. I consider it my first true prayer to God. Though it still pains me to sing this prayer, my pleas asking God to reveal himself to me were eventually answered. The more I prayed and laid bare my heart, the closer our relationship became. Had I not first sought God's help by honestly sharing what had been in my heart and mind, I might have continued in my lackluster, superficial faith.

God Wants an Intimate Relationship with You

A faulty image of God contributed to this tenuous relationship I had with him. As a child, I thought of God as a genie, and that prayer was like asking him to grant three wishes. As a teen, I thought of God as a judge, and that prayer was asking him to let me off the hook. Now as an adult, I finally understand God as he truly is—a loving, merciful Father with whom I can share my whole life. I realize I no longer must fear or hide in shame because he calls me by name and loved me into being.

Our image of God directly impacts how we relate to him. If you see God as a genie or a heavenly Santa Claus, your relationship with him becomes nothing more than a series of asks. If you see God as a judge, your relationship will be based on fear and, as a result, distant and cold. If you see God as an amorphous cloud, never to be reached or understood, your relationship with him may be nonexistent. These images of a distant God couldn't be more wrong.

God has wanted an intimate relationship with us from the very beginning, and this can be seen in his first interactions with Adam, the first human. In the Creation story, God and Adam converse. God talks to Adam, Adam responds, and vice versa. As always, God initiates the encounter. He tells Adam, "You are free to eat from any of the trees of the garden" (Genesis 2:16). God provides for Adam, responding to his needs. He notices that Adam is alone, and so, God creates a suitable partner. When Adam realizes what God has done, he exuberantly proclaims, "This one, at last, is bone of my bones and flesh of my flesh; This one shall be called 'woman,' for out of man this one has been taken" (Genesis 2:23). Adam freely shares with God what is on his mind and, more importantly, what is in his heart.

Adam had the beginnings of a great relationship with

God. He trusted him, confided in him, and listened to his voice. Adam, however, succumbed to temptation along with Eve. The allure of the serpent spurred doubts in the first man and woman. They began wondering if God was holding out on them. Why, they thought, can't they be "like gods" knowing the difference between right and wrong? They eat the forbidden fruit, blatantly disregarding God's guidance. When God calls out for them, they hide in shame, and suddenly what once was an open and loving relationship with God became closed, distant, and broken.

Sin, of course, is what caused the rift in the relationship between God and Adam, and sin continues to keep us far from God. Notice, however, who pulls away from the relationship when sin enters the picture. It isn't God who separates himself from Adam and Eve. Rather, it is they who separate themselves from God. When they began having doubts after talking to the serpent, they could have easily come to God. They could have plainly asked him, "God, why will we die if we eat from this tree? Why can't we acquire knowledge of good and evil?"

Adam and Eve's mistake is also our own. How often do we choose to hide our mistakes from God instead of coming to him and trusting in his mercy? God wants to be close to us, but our relationship with him depends on our choices. God doesn't expect perfection from us but rather, faithfulness.

Fortunately, we have Jesus, the New Adam, to show us what it means to have a personal, loving, ongoing relationship with God. No matter how busy or famous Jesus became, he made time to be with his Father. Jesus often fled from the crowds and even from his apostles to spend time alone with

God (Matthew 14:23, Mark 1:35, Luke 9:18). Jesus invites God to be part of his whole life by including his Father in every monumental event in his life. Jesus prays before raising Lazarus from the dead (John 11:41–44), during his baptism (Luke 3:21–22), and the multiplication of the loaves (Matthew 15:36), for example. Unlike Adam, Jesus doesn't hesitate to come to God with his fears, doubts, and temptations. On the night before his passion, Jesus fervently prayed, "My Father, if it is possible, let this cup pass from me; yet, not as I will, but as you will" (Matthew 26:39). Jesus' whole life was a prayer to God, and through him, we are given the perfect example of how we are called to enjoy intimacy with our Father.

Thus, prayer is the conduit through which we develop a personal and living relationship with Abba, our heavenly Father. Prayer is personal, requiring our whole heart. God invites us to share with him our joys, hopes, and frustrations—essentially our whole life—just as Jesus taught us. God is alive, and we can talk to him here and now. Prayer is a conversation with God, requiring us to speak and listen to him as exemplified by Adam and Jesus. If we want any relationship to be meaningful, we need to do both—listen and speak. The first step, however, is simply answering God's call when he knocks on our heart, letting the life-changing conversation begin.

Caution. Prayer Trap Ahead!
DRYNESS

I don't know what happened. My prayer life had been strong until recently. I used to love spending time with God. I would go to daily Mass to feel his peace and loving presence there. Now when I go, I don't feel anything at all. I'm so confused. Why do I suddenly feel so distant from God?

Tip 1: Switch things up. If you're experiencing dryness in prayer, reflect on how you pray. Have you fallen into a stale routine? Are you sharing the deepest part of yourself with God—your hopes, worries, and struggles—or do you share insignificant news with him, avoiding issues that God may be calling you to confront? Do you take time to listen to God?

Prayer is a *living* relationship with God. As such, our prayer life was meant to grow and change. If all you and your friend ever did together was bowl, your relationship could soon become predictable and uninteresting. In a few months you or your friend would be wanting to do something else. Similarly, we may experience dryness in our relationship with God, because our prayer life has become mechanical. Like all relationships, new experiences and challenges are needed for it to thrive and mature.

The good news is you can remedy this problem by switching things up. Try spending time with God in different ways. If you normally read the same prayer book every morning, try journaling or meditating on the lives of the saints for a change. If you have been praying the rosary every night, try reading Scripture or spending time in silence. Varying how you pray will allow you to experience God in exciting new ways.

Tip 2: Share your whole life with God. We all know the difference between an acquaintance and a close friend. If we sit near the former, we may talk about the weather and current events. If we sit next to the latter, we talk about our personal lives—marriage problems or a job promotion we have been praying about, for example. Our conversations with acquaintances may be short and dull, but our conversations with our closest friends are often substantial and lively.

Similarly, when we always pray by reading words from a page, hiding what is in our hearts and minds, our relationship with God is like a relationship with an acquaintance. It will be shallow and unsatisfying. When you pray, don't be afraid of sharing your whole life with God—most importantly, what is significant to you. He wants to hear about it all because he yearns to be part of it all.

Tip 3: Take time to listen to God. One-sided conversations aren't conversations at all. They are monologues. It is easy to feel distant from God and experience dryness in prayer when we give him no place in the relationship.

Strong relationships involve two parties, and giving God time to speak allows for fruitful dialogue. God desires to comfort, guide, and challenge you. He wants to respond to everything you have shared with him. When we truly allow ourselves to enter into a relationship with him, our lives are forever changed.

Therefore, give God the opportunity to respond to your needs. Listen for his voice in your life. You'll be amazed by the painstaking care God takes in addressing all the desires of your heart.

Tip 4: Act on your love for God, not on your feelings. "Love is patient, love is kind. It is not jealous, [love] is not pompous, it is not inflated, it is not rude, it does not seek its own interests, it is not quick-tempered, it does not brood over injury, it does not rejoice over wrongdoing but rejoices with the truth. It bears all things, believes all things, hopes all things, endures all things. Love never fails" (1 Corinthians 13:4–8).

Love is beautifully described in this widely quoted passage. It's a feeling *and* an action. Love is not about butter-flies in your stomach or the happiness you feel when you are with your beloved. When you love someone, you act patiently, kindly, selflessly, and honestly. True love is believing, hoping, and enduring all things. Love is a verb, not a noun. Love compels us to act and to demonstrate our love for another in the same way Christ loves us.

As such, we must let go of our expectations in prayer—especially the ones that involve how we should feel when we are with God. Even when we do not feel his presence and love for us, God has died on the cross for us and is present. When you persevere in prayer even amidst periods of dryness, you show God how much you love him and how important he is in your life.

Tip 5: Ask yourself why God is leading you here or what purpose this dryness serves. God has a plan for all things. The suffering we face, the confusion we experience, the frustrations we feel, can be used for his glory and your spiritual growth. If we allow it, everything we experience can serve a higher purpose. God takes our pain, struggles, and fears and tells us, "Behold, I make all things new" (Revelation 21:5).

The dryness we feel in prayer can also serve a higher purpose. It can spur us to experience God differently. It can strengthen our faith when we continually choose to remain in his presence, even when we do not feel him. Sometimes dryness compels a desire to understand God, drawing us closer to him as we make a greater effort to listen for his voice. In prayer, ask God how he is making "all things new" through this time of dryness while trusting that he forever remains within you.

God Meets You Where You Are

It seems impossible. How can we have a personal relationship with someone we cannot see, hear, or touch? I, too, didn't know how to speak to God. People would say, "Talk to God as if he were your friend." But it all felt so strange. You can see your friends—hug them, cry on their shoulder, or watch a movie with them. If I were to talk to God, it would feel as if I were talking into space and so, for much of my life, I never did.

When my friend spoke about God to my class, his demeanor was imbued with peace, joy, purpose, and confidence—qualities I lacked. I could tell he genuinely had a deep relationship with God. I, on the other hand, was frustrated with the monotony of life and couldn't figure out my purpose. What did my life mean? How was I supposed to live it? Does God really exist? Where does he fit into all of this?

It's interesting how God works. He uses the very thing he knows will reach us best to draw us closer. For me, it was music. The questions of faith I had were put to music, and that was what God used to help me speak to him. All God needed from me was openness to the possibility of his existence and a willingness to know him. He provided the rest.

That night I learned that God is never out of reach, and often he is right beside us. He initiates the conversation and knocks on our hearts. He meets us where we are. All God asks is that we are open to his loving presence, that we share what is on our minds and hearts, allowing the Holy Spirit to be our guide.

Let the Holy Spirit Guide You

Throughout the Bible, we see that the Holy Spirit works through us if we allow the Spirit to do so. In Matthew 4:1 "Jesus was led by the Spirit into the desert to be tempted by the devil." In Acts 16:14, we see that "the Lord opened [Lydia's] heart to pay attention to what Paul was saying." Saint Stephen, the Church's first martyr, "filled with the holy Spirit, looked up intently to heaven and saw the glory of God and Jesus standing at the right hand of God" (Acts 7:55).

These examples reveal that the Holy Spirit is a friend and advocate who leads us, already working on our behalf to make us more receptive to God's voice and, more importantly, to his divine love. The Holy Spirit dwells within us and helps us in our spiritual journey toward God. "The love of God has been poured out into our hearts through the Holy Spirit" (Romans 5:5), and this same Spirit prompts us to respond to God's love through prayer.

When I was trying to understand what God wanted me to do, the Holy Spirit drew my attention to what I enjoyed most—helping others strengthen their relationships with God, accompanying others in times of sorrow and joy, and sharing our beautiful faith with those he has called me to serve. The Holy Spirit helped me realize that all these gifts were essential to being a spiritual director. My conversation went something like this: "Holy Spirit, I know that you are calling me to be a spiritual director, but how is this supposed to happen?" In silence, I sensed that the Holy Spirit was calling me to first earn a degree in pastoral theology, receive more formation in spiritual direction, and then write.

When you pray, begin by invoking the Holy Spirit, as it

is the Holy Spirit who will help you tune into what is in your heart. Then, share with God all that is important to you.

True Prayer Comes from the Heart

The psalmists weren't afraid to come to God with a wide range of emotions such as sorrow, anger, and fear:

"My soul is depressed; / lift me up according to your word" (Psalm 119:28).

"Even though I walk through the valley of the shadow of death, / I will fear no evil, for you are with me; / your rod and your staff comfort me" (Psalm 23:4).

"Answer me when I call, my saving God. / When troubles hem me in, set me free; take pity on me, hear my prayer" (Psalm 4:2).

"I will praise you, LORD, with all my heart; / I will declare all your wondrous deeds" (Psalm 9:2).

These verses illustrate how prayers should come from our hearts. Many people feel as if they must filter what they say in prayer to God, but there is no need. God already knows what we are going through. He accepts your tears and sorrows. He celebrates with you when you are joyful and cries with you when you are in pain.

Whether you are questioning his existence, discerning his call, desiring more closeness to him, or seeking something else, pray about it. Share what is in your heart. Whether it is spoken, sung, written, or even a screamed heartache, God hears you. The more you seek him, the more he will reveal himself to you.

For Practice and Reflection

God wants to hear from you. Today, speak to God with your whole heart through an improvised prayer. This is just what it sounds like—a prayer that hasn't been prepared by someone else. There are no rules. All that is required is that you share whatever the Holy Spirit is inspiring you to express to God. To start, try reflecting on these questions: *What has been on your mind and in your heart lately? What are you seeking from God right now?* Find a quiet place and take time to share it with God. Remember, there is no "right" way to pray so long as it comes from your heart, even if it is "God, I need you today. Please be with me!" or "Jesus, help me to draw closer to you!"

∾

The personal experiences and examples of others can inspire our faith. Think of a time when you were inspired to draw closer to God. Was it something you read, heard, saw, or experienced?

Prayer is a personal, loving, ongoing relationship with God. What has your prayer life been like, and how may God be inviting you into a more intimate relationship?

What are you seeking from God at this moment? Do you feel comfortable sharing this with God in prayer?

CHAPTER 2

Inviting God into Every Part of Your Life

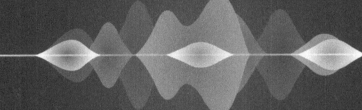

"We must speak to God as a friend speaks to his friend, servant to his master; now asking some favor, now acknowledging our faults, and communicating to him all that concerns us, our thoughts, our fears, our projects, our desires, and in all things seeking his counsel."

ST. IGNATIUS OF LOYOLA

In any relationship, honesty and vulnerability are required for it to flourish and persist. This is especially the case in our relationship with God. God desires to hear from us—not only when we need something but also, when we are lonely, happy, sad, bored, tired, frustrated, bewildered, overwhelmed, and the like. God desires to be involved in our *whole* lives, not just pieces of it.

Are you frustrated because you can't seem to find a job that recognizes your gifts and abilities? Let God know. Are you afraid of not being able to provide for your family? Share this with him. Are you angry with God because you feel he doesn't really care about your needs? Perhaps you blame him for the death of someone close to you? Don't hold back. Let him know of your anger toward him. God can take it.

Some may ask, "Well, what's the point of sharing all of this? How can expressing my anger or doubts toward God be helpful?" Whatever you may be feeling, whatever you may be going through, God wants to be part of it all. As you can see in the following example, sharing these feelings with God through frequent, persistent prayer can change the course of your life. It certainly changed mine.

Sharing Our Doubts with God

After dating for almost two years, my boyfriend AJ and I were at the brink of breaking up. We decided we would finally talk about our problems that night, and so, once AJ parked the car in the driveway, we both just sat there...in utter silence. Our eyes avoided each other. My hands were sweaty, and I couldn't help but feel overwhelming sadness at this moment. I thought to myself, *Would this be the end of us? What did we do wrong?*

After minutes that felt like years of excruciating silence, AJ finally spoke: "I feel as if you don't really love and care for me as much as I love and care for you. Are you even attracted to me? You seem to be uncomfortable with physical affection even though all I am doing is giving you a hug or a kiss."

I felt my face flush. "How could you think that?" I asked. "Of course, I love you, and I wouldn't be dating you if I wasn't attracted to you. I'm just not used to showing my love for others physically. I'm so sorry. I didn't know you felt this way. I think we just have different ways of showing our love for each other, and we need to learn how the other best receives love."

AJ sat in concentration. "There is one thing that really frustrates me," I said. "You can go weeks, sometimes months, festering over something that has hurt you before sharing it with me. It really worries me when you do this, because in these moments, I wonder why we are even together when you just look so miserable with me."

AJ straightened up and with a look of deep concern said, "I'm so sorry. Yes, I know I tend to regress inward when I'm confused and hurt. It's just that I've been so lost in our relationship that I don't know what to do, how to act, or even what to say."

"How about the truth?" I quickly interjected. "Just like how you get frustrated with me when I don't tell you what is bothering me right away, I need to know what is going on in your head—and preferably within a week. Not in a few weeks and definitely not in a few months. Do you think we can agree to that?"

AJ nodded and said, "Yeah, that seems fair."

After discussing our concerns and grievances for another hour, I finally asked, "So, where are we now? Do you think we should continue on in our relationship?"

"I don't know. It's been two years since we started dating. Shouldn't we know by now if we are right for each other?" he said sadly.

"I guess. I'm not sure, either," I replied. "Why don't we pray about it? I heard about the fifty-four-day novena prayer just recently, and it's supposed to help you understand God's will for anything you ask. Maybe we can pray this every night and ask Mother Mary to intercede on our behalf regarding whether it's God's will for us to stay together. After the fifty-four days are over, we can discuss what we heard from God regarding our relationship. What do you think? Do you want to try it?"

"Yeah, let's try it," AJ said. "I hope it will give us some clarity."

For fifty-four days, AJ and I prayed the rosary. If we were together, we would pray it at the end of our date night. If we were apart, we would pray it over the phone.

I also prayed separately to God. I confided in him about

the confusion I felt. As I shared my heartache with God, tears would cascade down my cheeks, dampening my pillow. "God, why can't we seem to understand each other?" I would ask. "Why is it so hard for us to be in a relationship with each other?" Oftentimes, I was met with silence, left alone to ponder.

The more we prayed, however, the more we understood what God was calling us to do. For us to improve our relationship, we needed to put our insecurities and fears aside. We had to be completely open with each other about our thoughts, feelings, and needs. The anxiety-ridden conversation we had in the car was surprisingly the most open discussion we had had until then. We had both bottled up our feelings for so long that they were starting to turn into deep resentments. Fortunately, the concerns we raised were fixable, and we were both willing to put in the effort to address each other's needs. When we finished the fifty-four-day novena, we were at peace and feeling confident in our decision to continue dating.

God Wants to be Part of It All

Although this time of discernment was difficult for us, it brought us closer to God, because we continually sought his guidance and healing through it all. When we began despairing, his word in sacred Scripture gave us hope. God was present in our doubts and confusion, and it was he who ultimately brought us back together through prayer.

AJ and I were angry with each other when we had that conversation in the car. Expressing these feelings, however, gave us the chance to apologize and address each other's concerns. This, in turn, helped us to grow in understanding and compassion for one another. In the same way, when we speak frankly to God, we are giving him the opportunity to respond to our prayers. Through prayer we welcome him into our lives and invite him to speak.

There are five basic types of prayers: petition, intercession, thanksgiving, praise, and blessing and adoration. But no matter what prayer type you use, the key is to be open and honest with God.

Prayer of Petition

What are you struggling with at this moment? What would you like God to help you with?

When we come to God with our needs, we are offering a prayer of petition. We ask, plead, and cry out to God for forgiveness, healing, understanding, guidance, peace, or anything else we might need. "When we share in God's saving love, we understand that *every need* can become the object of petition" (*Catechism of the Catholic Church*, 2633), and for this reason it is the prayer form that we are most familiar with.

Hannah, one of Elkanah's wives, desperately begged God to bless her with a child (1 Samuel 1:1–28). After years of being barren, Hannah was the object of ridicule by Elkanah's other wife, Peninnah, who had many children. Peninnah's continual torment of Hannah's barrenness would provoke Hannah into depression. After another day of Peninnah's cruel taunting, Hannah fled to the temple in tears. She cried out to God in hopes that he would hear her plea and remember her. When Eli, one of the priests, saw her in her hysterical state, he immediately thought she was drunk and admonished her. Hannah protested and said to Eli, "I am an unhappy woman. I have had neither wine nor liquor; I was only pouring out my heart to the LORD. Do not think your servant a worthless woman; my prayer has been prompted by my deep sorrow and misery" (1 Samuel 1:15–16).

Whenever I read Hannah's response to Eli, I am reminded of how God calls us to run to him, like children to their parents, bringing every need we have. Hannah prayed with the greatest fervor, baring her pain, frustration, and despair to God. She left nothing hidden and entrusted her suffering and deepest longing to God, having faith that he would listen. Several days later, Hannah conceived. God *was* listening, and he answered her prayer by blessing her with a son.

Prayer of Intercession

Who in your life are you concerned about?

When we pray for others, we are interceding on their behalf. We ask God to help our parent find a job. We tell him about our friend who is suffering with a mental illness and in need of healing. We plead with God to comfort our sister who has just lost her husband. "Asking on behalf of another has been characteristic of a heart attuned to God's mercy" (*CCC* 2635). We become more like Christ who intercedes on behalf of us all, putting our self-interest aside.

When the centurion's servant fell gravely ill, he approached Jesus and expressed his great concern and sorrow for his servant's painful, debilitating condition (Matthew 8:5–13). He saw the immense agony his loyal servant was going through and it compelled him to action. In his mercy, the centurion could not sit idly by while his servant lay in anguish. He intercedes on the servant's behalf, and when Jesus agrees to heal the servant, the centurion says, "Lord, I am not worthy to have you enter under my roof; only say the word and my servant will be healed" (Matthew 8:8). Jesus publicly praises the centurion for his strong faith, and when the centurion returns home, he finds his servant healed—just as he knew he would.

Like Hannah, the centurion came to God, freely sharing everything on his mind and in his heart. He entrusted his friend and servant to Jesus, honoring his greatness and power. As a result, the centurion's mercy, humility, and faith became the vehicle through which God miraculously cured his servant.

Prayer of Thanksgiving

What blessings would you like to thank him for?

When we express gratitude to God for all he has done, we are saying a prayer of thanksgiving. "Every joy and suffering, every event and need can become the matter for thanksgiving which, sharing in that of Christ, should fill one's whole life" (*CCC* 2648). Gratitude is the way we acknowledge the generosity and love of God. Our health, our home, the food on our table, our family, our jobs, our breath and being, become opportunities to speak to God. We come to realize that God is the giver of all these good gifts and that the only appropriate response is to give thanks.

As Jesus came to a village to rest from his journey to Jerusalem, ten lepers came to him, imploring him to cure them of their disease (Luke 17:11–19). Jesus took pity on the lepers and healed them. "And one of them, realizing he had been healed, returned, glorifying God in a loud voice; and he fell at the feet of Jesus and thanked him" (Luke 17:15–16). Jesus blesses this particular leper, because of the ten Jesus healed, only he came back to give thanks.

Leprosy leaves sufferers with severely disfigured skin. Unfortunately, this is only one of its many effects. Leprosy was highly stigmatized. People feared being near sufferers, as they believed that leprosy was extremely contagious. Lepers were considered unclean, repulsive, and cursed, and so they were isolated from the community. As such, leprosy affected the victims' whole lives—their health, social status, self-esteem, and employability, to name a few.

Why, then, would the other nine not come back to thank Jesus? He not only cured them of their disease but changed their whole lives! Suddenly, all the doors that were once closed to them were opened. Perhaps they were so ecstatic to be free of the disease and its stigma that they just forgot. They were too busy enjoying their newfound health to remember the source of their liberation. The one person who was cured, however, did not take the precious gift of healing for granted. He fell at Jesus' feet to thank him, and his faith saved him. The leper's gratitude drew him closer to God, bringing even more blessings upon him.

Prayer of Praise

What would you like to praise God for? How has he filled your life with awe and wonder?

When we tell God how much we respect, admire, and honor him, we are offering a prayer of praise. "Prayer of praise is entirely disinterested and rises to God, lauds him, and gives him glory for his own sake, quite beyond what he has done, but simply because HE IS" (*CCC* 2649). Our praises are the way we show God that he is God. We remember that he is the Creator and source of all life and that we are only his creatures who were born out of his great love for us. We share with God our awe in all that he has created. We pause to praise him for his unending mercy. We express to God our uncontainable joy at his goodness.

The Magnificat is a beautiful example of a prayer of praise. Mary says to her cousin, Elizabeth, "My soul proclaims the greatness of the Lord; my spirit rejoices in God my savior. For he has looked upon his handmaid's lowliness;   behold, from now on will all ages call me blessed. The Mighty One has done great things for me, and holy is his name" (Luke 1:46–49). Mary and Elizabeth were both blessed with miraculous pregnancies. Mary conceived through the power of the Holy Spirit, and Elizabeth conceived in her old age. When Mary approaches and greets Elizabeth, Elizabeth's baby leaps in her womb. The baby senses that the Lord is near, and indeed he is through Mary.

Mary praises God for all that he has done in her life and that of others. She recognizes his greatness and enthusiastically glorifies his name. Mary is full of joy, and she rightfully honors God who is the source of it. Through her prayer of praise, she expresses the great awe and wonderment she has for him.

Prayer of Blessing and Adoration

How are you being inspired to bless and adore God today?

When we take time to worship, cherish, bless, and love God, we are offering a prayer of blessing and adoration. It is an intimate encounter with God in which we accept the blessings he has showered upon us and bless him in return (*CCC* 2626). We bow before God, giving him homage as the Magi once did before the Baby Jesus (Matthew 2:11). We stay close beside him, enjoying his presence. We bask in God's love and hold him close.

When Martha was busy doing all the serving for Jesus and the apostles, her sister Mary sat near Jesus' feet, listening to him speak. As the night wore on, Martha became increasingly anxious and asked Jesus to speak to Mary about helping her with the serving. Jesus, however, responds to Martha affirming her sister's choice of focusing her whole attention on him by saying, "Martha, Martha, you are anxious and worried about many things. There is need of only one thing. Mary has chosen the better part and it will not be taken from her" (Luke 10:41–42).

Like Mary, we are called to sit at the feet of Jesus and listen attentively to his voice in our lives. When we take this posture, we are respectfully remaining silent in his holy presence (*CCC* 2628). We put aside anything that may distract us from being fully present to him, and through this prayer of adoration and blessing we share our deep love for God.

Share What Is Important to You

Hannah, the centurion, the leper, and Mary, the sister of Martha, entrusted God with their needs, having faith that he would fulfill every desire of their heart. Through these forms of prayer, they allowed God to draw close to them. They trusted in his mercy and love, understanding that God knew what was best for them.

We can learn from their earnest prayers because God simply desires to hear what is most important to us. He wants to hear about your hopes and dreams. He wants to know about your fears and failures. God wants to know about your day—what happened, what inspired you, the people you spoke to, the situations that annoyed you, and anything else significant to you.

Lucas, one of the young adults in our parish, is a great example of someone who faithfully invites God in every part of his life. As one of our newest youth ministry team leaders, he felt unworthy to serve the youth of our parish. He thought he didn't know enough about the Bible, that his prayer life was inadequate, and that he wasn't the best example of what a youth leader should be. In prayer, Lucas shared these sentiments with God asking him to affirm his calling to serve the parish youth. Weeks later, Lucas was overjoyed when he heard a speaker say, "God does not call the equipped but equips the called." He knew immediately that God was reassuring him, and that God would give him all he needed to be an effective leader.

When Lucas was struggling in college, he didn't hesitate to ask God for help. "God, I just can't seem to manage all of my classes," he prayed. "I have two essays due next week. I have a final on Friday and a project due on Monday. I don't know how I am going to get all of this done, and I'm feeling so overwhelmed." Lucas continued asking God for help with school every night that week. Soon he realized that God was urging him to reassess his priorities. Lucas decided to work fewer hours at his part-time job and cut time-wasters like social media and television until he caught up with his studies.

When Lucas' mother gave birth to a second child, he beamed with excitement. Until then, Lucas was an only child who had longed for this moment. "God, you continue to amaze me!" he prayed. "Thank you for the gift of my little brother! Please be with my mother and give her the rest and healing she needs to best care for Noah. And please be with me, that I may be a good brother."

Lucas shared with God what was most important to him. He told God what was going on in his life, and he came to God with his needs, joys, thanksgiving, and praise. Let us follow in his example and welcome God into all aspects of our lives, leaving nothing unsaid.

For Practice and Reflection

God wants to draw closer to you. Speak to him through journaling, holding nothing back. Journaling is a great way to share your thoughts and feelings with God. It often may be difficult for us to express our hurt, shame, fear, or other deep-seated emotions aloud. Writing it, however, can help bring clarity to a difficult situation, and it gives us an opportunity to record how God has answered our prayers through the years. If we struggle to believe God cares for us, for example, we can look back in our journal and remember the times when we recognized his loving hand working in us. Write what you would like to say to God following these steps:

1. On a blank piece of paper or journal, write "Dear God" at the top of the page. Then, share with God whatever you feel called to express. It could be about how you are feeling, any intentions you may have, things you want to thank him for, what happened throughout your day, or anything else the Holy Spirit is calling you to share with God at that moment.

2. On another piece of paper or on another page of your journal, write "Dear (your own name)." Here, prayerfully reflect on what you think God would say in response to what you shared with him in your letter. People sometimes struggle with this part. They ask, "How can I know what God would

say back to me?" In the next few chapters, you will learn what God's voice sounds like, and this will help you when you journal. For now, listen closely to the Holy Spirit who lives within you and write what you sense God would say to you.

~~~

What was the most honest conversation you have ever had with someone? What happened and what issues were resolved?

Our relationship with God requires the same level of vulnerability and honesty as any other important relationship. What is your relationship with God like? How easy or difficult has it been to invite God into every part of your life?

Can you think of a time when you shared something of great importance with God? What did you tell him and how did he respond?

CHAPTER 3

Opening Your Ears and Heart to God

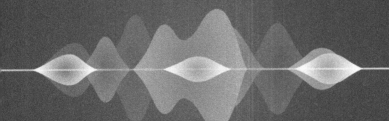

> "When it's God who is speaking...the proper way to behave is to imitate someone who has an irresistible curiosity and who listens at keyholes. You must listen to everything God says at the keyhole of your heart."
>
> **ST. JOHN VIANNEY**

Saint Ignatius of Loyola had money and power. He dreamed of fame and chased glory. He was a great military leader motivated by heroism, but one fateful day changed it all. During a battle against the French, a cannonball struck Ignatius in the leg, leaving him badly wounded and on a long, arduous road to recovery. To occupy his time, he read the only books that were available: a small library on the life of Christ and the saints. As he read, his heart, mind, and spirit began to change. Ignatius noticed that while he reflected on his worldly desires of fame and fortune, the happiness he felt lasted but a short time. However, when he reflected on the virtues and selfless love of Christ and the saints, the joy and inspiration he felt remained within him indefinitely. God spoke to Ignatius through spiritual reading, his life was transformed, and he inspired change in others.

A woman of our time, St. Teresa of Calcutta also was a life changer and one of the most remarkable women of any era. She gave generously, lived righteously, and loved deeply. Teresa valued and upheld the dignity of all, especially those seen as "untouchables." She cared for the dying in the slums and the poorest of the poor by washing their wounds, teaching their children, comforting the dying, and sharing the joy and love of Christ through her compassionate presence. While those around her saw nothing but light, Teresa felt as if she was being suffocated by an enveloping darkness. Though she was once graced with visions and a profound intimacy with God, Teresa spent the remainder of her life in darkness and silence from the One she loved most. Even though she knew that God had not left her, she felt that it was so. Teresa felt like the untouchables she served—unloved, unwanted, abandoned, and lost. She experienced feelings of worthlessness for decades, and some say she lived with this darkness until the day she died. God, however, was speaking to her through the darkness and in the silence, and Teresa came to realize that she was being given the opportunity to share in the desolation of the poor she served.

One of my directees is a ministry coordinator. He resigned from a more lucrative secular job to work full time in ministry. He suffers from depression, self-doubt, and anxiety. He often feels as if his life is at a standstill. To him it seems as if most people his age are already set in their careers, married to the loves of their life, and caring for their children. Yet he is still discerning how God is calling him to serve in ministry, what his vocation will be, and whether he will be a father some day. When he begins thinking of the unsettled aspects of his life, it leads him into a downward spiral of depression. However, he has a fervent faith in God. When I ask him how God speaks to him during difficult times, he shares that it is through adoration and the Mass that God will console him and give him peace. "Whenever I sit in front of the Blessed Sacrament, God reminds me that I am not alone, that I am worthy, and that I am loved," he says. "I feel his presence and know that he is already healing me."

One of the young adults in our ministry group is a dedicated teacher, self-taught salsa dancer, and devoted follower of Jesus Christ. She has an infectious laugh and a zest for life. If you need to reach her, you are sure to find her in one of two places: a salsa club or church. Her life changed when one of her friends asked her to come to a Bible study, where she heard and understood the words, "God loves you!" She enjoys watching movies so much that I was compelled to make a request that would set her on a new path: "Would you consider leading a ministry based off of movies?" She said she would think about it. A year later, she accepted, and a new ministry was born. Once a month, she would select a film for our group to watch, helping us to hear what God may be saying to each of us through a line, character, or theme from the movie.

God Responds
to Our Every Prayer

Many people find talking to God easier than listening to God. After all, how can you possibly listen to someone you cannot see, hear, or touch? The comments I get the most are: "It feels as if I am talking to thin air; is he really listening?" "I pray all the time, but nothing happens." "Do I even matter to him?"

While we may not perceive God in accustomed ways, God *can* be seen, he *can* be heard, and yes, he *can* even be touched. God can be seen through everything and everyone he has created. He can be heard through the sacred Scripture he inspired, the Mass he instituted, the people he formed, and in so many other ways. He can be touched through the Eucharist and through the loved ones he has placed in your life. Moreover, his presence can be felt within your very being because God the Holy Spirit dwells within you.

Contrary to what some believe, God can and does respond to our hopes, dreams, frustrations, anger, sadness, and anything else we may share with him in prayer. God has created you in his image and likeness (Genesis 1:27). He knows the number of hairs on your head (Luke 12:7) and willingly sacrificed his Son so that you might live (John 3:16). He cries with you if you have suffered a miscarriage. He carries you when you are too ill to stand. He laughs with you when your toddler manages to climb out of the crib and onto your bed. He shares in your joy when you finally meet the love of your life. He supports you when you have nearly reached your breaking point. God is with you, and he desires to be part of every area of your life. He hears you, he thirsts for you, and he loves you.

All the aforementioned people heard God speak to them in different, profound ways. They experienced his great love for them, and when they poured out their hearts to him, he listened and responded. They sought him in Scripture, at Mass, in adoration, and through spiritual reading, for example. They included God in their lives and attentively waited to hear God's voice in response to their prayers.

In the same way, we are called to open our ears and heart to God. When we pray, we should talk to God with faith that he is listening and trusting that he will answer. This means that we should be continually on the lookout for the ways in which he may be communicating back to us. To better hear God's voice, keep this in mind:

Make Time to Listen

How often do you spend time with an acquaintance? Once a week? Twice a month? Once a year during a birthday celebration? Never?

How much time do you spend with a close friend, parent, or sibling?

Now, compare these two types of relationships with your significant other, spouse, or religious community. How often do you spend time with them?

Do you notice any differences in the time spent with these various groups of people in your life? For most, the closer you are (or desire to become) with someone is directly proportional to the amount of time you spend with them. And, the more time you spend with your significant others, the closer that relationship becomes. We show how important people are in our lives by carving out time for them.

The more time we spend with God, the more opportunities we have to hear his voice and the closer our relationship with him becomes. God is continually speaking to us, but often we are too busy to listen. We have work, school, kids to take care of, errands to run, our favorite TV shows to watch, concerts to attend, friends to have dinner with, laundry to fold, not to mention that darned treadmill we have been meaning to exercise on. When does anyone find the time to be with God?

Just like with the most significant people in our lives, we *make* time. We compare calendars to see what day and time works best. We plan, and if we get busy, we make sure to schedule time to be together regardless of how short the visit may be. If all else fails and life gets too hectic to spend time with someone in our lives, we take a step back and see what we may need to drop to make life more manageable. This is what we are called to do with God.

So, when is the best time for you to be with God? Is it thirty minutes every morning before work? Is it during your lunch break at school? Is it Tuesday and Thursday afternoons when your kids are at baseball practice? Schedule it on your calendar and honor it. After all, the best dates you could ever go on are the ones with God!

When I asked my youth and young-adult leaders how they made time to listen to God in prayer, their responses were surprisingly varied. One of my wonderful parent volunteers shared that she would go to Mass every morning, and this helped her to start the day right. One of my young adults will write in her prayer journal every night before sleeping and ask God to help her see the blessings of that day. A youth leader said he would sit before the Blessed Sacrament and ask the Holy Spirit for help with confusing areas in his life. These leaders creatively incorporated prayer in their everyday lives, and though everyone gets busy, they make time to both speak and listen to God.

Caution. Prayer Trap Ahead!
BUSYNESS

It's so hard for me to find time to be with God. With work, school, and my children, I barely have time for myself! I want to have a stronger relationship with God, but I don't know how to make it work. What should I do?

Tip 1: Make time to pray. Just like we make time to exercise, watch a child's basketball game, go on a date, or go to a party, we are called to make time for God no matter how brief that time may be in the beginning. This could mean you are called to make some sacrifices to clear out time for God. For example, you might need to cut ten or twenty minutes from your TV or social-media time each day. What may God be urging you to cut back on so you can spend more time with him? Once you have figured it out, replace that time with prayer and make sure to mark your "dates" with God on your calendar. Set a reminder on your phone.

Tip 2: Listen to Catholic podcasts. Catholic podcasts are amazing because you can listen to them while you are running, walking, driving, or doing chores. These podcasts come in many forms: homilies by inspiring priests, reflections on Bible readings, meditations like the rosary and Divine Mercy Chaplet, talks by Catholic speakers on spiritual living, and more. Podcasts can be effective ways to hear God's voice. They can be a source of spiritual and moral edification, healing, hope, and love. Catholic podcasts are perfect for active and busy Christians because they are portable. Just insert your earbuds and allow God's voice to come through while you run or garden. It's amazing how much you'll grow in holiness by tuning in.

Tip 3: Pray while you work. Prayer is simply spending time with God—being with him, listening to him, talking to him, walking with him, and yes, even being at work with him. Think of prayer as an activity that's as natural as breathing because God is truly present everywhere, in everyone, and at every moment. While you are brushing your teeth, for example, ask God to help make you clean. When you are picking up your child from school, thank God for always being there to raise you up whenever you need him or need a ride to heaven. When a coworker or client is frustrating you, call to mind the patience, love, and mercy God has for you and try to emulate him. Each moment, no matter how busy you are, can be an opportunity to call to mind our loving Father who wants to be with you here and now.

Invoke the Holy Spirit

Prayer may seem daunting at first, but God has already equipped us with the tools we need to communicate with him through his Spirit. The Holy Spirit is the key to prayer because it opens us to hear God's voice speaking within us. The Holy Spirit "comes to the aid of our weakness; for we do not know how to pray as we ought, but the Spirit itself intercedes with inexpressible groanings" (Romans 8:26). The Spirit speaks on our behalf and attunes us to the presence of God working in our lives.

The story of Philip and the Ethiopian highlights how the Holy Spirit directs our time of prayer and compels us to act according to his words. When Philip was traveling from Jerusalem to Gaza, he saw an Ethiopian eunuch seated in his chariot reading Isaiah. The Holy Spirit said to Philip, "Go and join up with that chariot" (Acts 8:29). Philip runs to the Ethiopian and helps him understand the passage he was reading. The Ethiopian, inspired by Philip's words, asks Philip to baptize him.

Philip, a man devoted to prayer, was continually ready with ears opened to hear and respond to God's call. He invited God to speak to him all day long, and so, when the Holy Spirit told Philip to join the chariot, Philip had no trouble hearing the Spirit's voice. We also must invite God the Holy Spirit to join our time of prayer.

When you wish to hear God's voice, begin with an invocation to the Holy Spirit. It could be as simple as saying, "Holy Spirit, help me to hear what you may be trying to tell me through this (Scripture passage, church song, homily, spiritual book, as examples). Amen." Then, as you pray, actively meditate on the question: *How might God be speaking to me through this?* Invoking the Holy Spirit in this way will help center your time of prayer and remind you to actively listen to God who yearns to speak to you.

Get Away from the Noise

Have you ever tried to have a conversation with someone during a concert or at a nightclub? It's safe to say that meaningful conversations don't often happen at these places. Why? All the noise, of course. This is what distractions are—noise. If we truly want to hear God, we must escape the noise that prevents us from doing just that.

Cell phones. Television. Movies. Work. People. Social media. Computers. Music. Video games. Sports. Food. Parties. Hobbies. These aren't necessarily bad things, and some could be considered essential to a normal life. However, if any of them distract you from being present physically, mentally, and spiritually from your time with God, then it would be best to step away from them during times of prayer. For example, you could choose a time when your children are asleep or simply turn off your television when you pray.

Everyone is different. What distracts one person may help another. A smartphone, for instance, may aid a person in prayer if he or she is using it to read a Scripture verse or research the biography of a saint. However, if a person is too easily tempted to answer text messages or calls during prayer, having a phone handy may not be a good idea. A simple rule of thumb is, if it aids you in prayer, use it. If it distracts you from prayer, step away from it.

Seek God's Voice

We were hopelessly lost. My family and I were enjoying the sights and sounds of Florence, Italy, until we took one too many turns before our next destination—the Cathedral of Santa Maria del Fiore. After wandering aimlessly for some time, my dad stopped a passerby: "Hello, sir," he said. "My family and I are lost. Could you help us find the church?"

Unfortunately, the passerby responded in a language we couldn't understand. With determination, my dad looked at the man and started gesturing as he spoke. "We are" (pointing to all of us) "looking for" (putting his right hand above his brow) "the church" (he exclaimed as he fell to his knees and made the Sign of the Cross).

The passerby laughed heartily, responding: *"Chiesa?"*

Yes! Finally, the word we were searching for: "church" in Italian. We nodded appreciatively, and the man pointed the way we needed to go. Needless to say, we were no longer lost.

So often we miss out on what God may be telling us simply because we do not understand his language. Like the scene with my father and the passerby, we expect God to speak a certain language. Maybe you envision God speaking to you through a burning bush like Moses or in your dreams like Joseph. Maybe you expect God to speak to you through very specific signs. For example, *If I get this job, then I know God is listening and cares for me.* God's language or way of speaking, however, is multifaceted and unique to each person. We cannot confine ourselves to any single way God could possibly communicate with us, because to do so would only limit our understanding of him.

My father learned that he had to discover another way to communicate with the passerby: gesturing. Similarly, if we are to better understand God, we must expand our knowledge of the ways he chooses to communicate. I devote the next few chapters to helping you with this very task. These chapters will reveal how God often speaks through Scripture, silence, traditional, and nontraditional means. If we truly want to hear his loving, transformative voice in our lives, then we must faithfully seek him through these "languages" in prayer.

For Practice and Reflection

God yearns to speak to you. Listen to his voice through meditation. To meditate simply means to focus our thoughts on God. We can use a Bible passage, a prayer, or any spiritual work to reflect on. When we meditate, we think about what we are reading—what it means, how it makes us feel, how it relates to us, and more importantly, what God may be trying to communicate to us through it. Allow God to speak to your soul by praying the Peace Prayer attributed St. Francis below. Read each line slowly, pausing to think and reflect on what each line means to you.

Lord, make me an instrument of your peace:
where there is hatred, let me sow love;
where there is injury, pardon;
where there is doubt, faith;
where there is despair, hope;
where there is darkness, light;
where there is sadness, joy.
O divine Master, grant that I may not so much seek
to be consoled as to console,
to be understood as to understand,
to be loved as to love.
For it is in giving that we receive,
it is in pardoning that we are pardoned,
and it is in dying that we are born to eternal life.
Amen.

≋

Of the four vignettes described at the beginning of the chapter, which account most affected you and why?

Have you ever heard God speak to you? If so, how did he speak to you and what did he say?

Of the common prayer distractions noted in this chapter, which one distracts you in prayer, and what can you do to avoid these distractions when spending time with God?

CHAPTER 4

God Speaks through Sacred Scripture

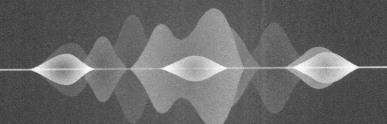

> "Ignorance of Scripture is ignorance of Christ!"
>
> **ST. JEROME**

Journal entry, November 28, 2009:

Why am I Catholic? Why do I believe in God? I can't see, touch, hear, or embrace God, so why follow him? Ever since I received the sacrament of confirmation, I've pondered these questions and wondered what pulls me to continue believing amidst these doubts. It almost feels like I question God's existence every day. I can't help but think: Is God real?

Distinguishing God's Voice

Looking back on the pages of my journal, I am reminded of the pivotal role sacred Scripture played in my conversion. Before I began reading the Bible, my faith and relationship with God was nonexistent. As I prayed with sacred Scripture, however, my understanding of who God is and what his voice sounds like became clearer.

Have you ever heard a rumor about one of your best friends and thought to yourself, *Hmm...that doesn't sound like something she (he) would do.* You immediately call your friend, and sure enough, it was a vicious lie started by a jealous coworker. You were able to distinguish between truth and gossip because you've spent years getting to know your friend. You know what she likes and dislikes. You know the type of person she is and what values she upholds. Those who didn't know your friend well enough, though, were fooled into believing the rumor was true.

Similarly, it is hard to hear and distinguish God's voice when we don't know what he sounds like. Opposing voices can quickly confuse us, and that is why taking the time to get to know God by reading Scripture is vital to understanding which voice is his. When we meditate on Bible passages, the answer becomes clear—the voice of love and mercy is undoubtedly God's voice. His voice is uplifting, kind, patient, healing, challenging, and compassionate. When Christ spoke in the Gospels, the lives and hearts of those who heard and adopted his messages were transformed in positive, meaningful ways.

When I was in high school, I struggled with feeling I wasn't good enough. Magazines and TV shows portrayed beautiful women with flawless figures and gorgeous faces. These voices in the media weren't ashamed to tell me I had to look, dress, and act in a particular way to gain the approval of others. It wasn't until I read Song of Songs 4:7 that I realized just how wrong these voices were. It proclaims, "You are beautiful in every way, my friend, there is no flaw in you!" God was reminding me through this verse that I am enough and loved just the way I am.

When I was in college, I developed a crush on an atheist. As I prayed about whether I should date him, I was led to 1 Corinthians 7:12–13 which reads, "To the rest I say (not the Lord)...if any woman has a husband who is an unbeliever, and he is willing to go on living with her, she should not divorce her husband. For the unbelieving husband is made holy through his wife." Through Scripture, God revealed to me that I had nothing to fear about dating others who had different beliefs than mine. I sensed that God wanted me to discern for myself what I truly wanted in a relationship and, after dating him, I realized that I yearned to be with someone who shared my faith with me and brought me closer to God. I would have never known this had God not encouraged me through Scripture to give my classmate a chance.

When I graduated from college, I was rejected numerous times from the career path I was working toward. Feeling confused and frustrated, I took time in prayer, opened the Bible, and read words spoken by God: "For I know well the plans I have in mind for you...plans for your welfare and not for woe, so as to give you a future of hope" (Jeremiah 29:11). God had something greater in mind for me, a plan I was unaware of because I was too busy forging my own path. As I turned my gaze toward God, I learned that he was calling me to serve full-time in ministry—first as a youth and young-adult minister, and then as a spiritual director. None of these paths had ever crossed my mind, and had I not trusted in God's plans for me through his word, I would have missed out on both life-changing opportunities to serve in ministry.

Through sacred Scripture, God responded to my prayers and spoke directly to me. His word gave me insight into who I was—his most precious daughter. His word gave me guidance when I was confused, and his word gave me encouragement when I felt like I had failed. God desires to speak to you through Scripture, too, and our knowledge and understanding of the Bible is crucial if we truly wish to hear his voice guiding us in our everyday lives. As Christians, we view the whole Bible through the lens of the New Testament (especially the Gospels), because they eloquently reveal the life, teachings, and passion of Christ. If reading the Bible is daunting for you, begin there and allow God to speak to you through his Son.

God's Word Defends Us Against Temptation

When Jesus was tempted in the desert, he relied on Scripture to counter the devil's lies (Matthew 4:1–11). After fasting forty days, Jesus was famished. The devil taunted Jesus to turn stones into bread to prove he was the Son of God. But Jesus wasn't easily fooled. He refuses, replying with Scripture: "It is not by bread alone that people live, but by all that comes forth from the mouth of the LORD" (Deuteronomy 8:3).

In an attempt to mislead Jesus, the devil distorts Scripture to tempt Christ to throw himself over the temple wall since it is written that angels would save him. Jesus admonishes the devil using Deuteronomy 6:16: "You shall not put the Lord, your God, to the test." Then the devil promises Jesus riches and power over all the kingdoms in the world if Jesus worships him. Still, Jesus stood firm and refused the devil's false promises proclaiming, "The Lord, your God, shall you fear; him shall you serve" (Deuteronomy 6:13).

For me, reading about the temptation of Jesus, is like watching a tennis match. The devil serves, Jesus hits a forehand, the devil returns with a lob, and Jesus moves forward executing a brilliant overhead smash. While it may first appear as if Jesus is always playing defense, he is never caught off guard by the devil. When the devil serves his first shot, Jesus doesn't have to give the devil's temptation a second thought. Jesus' thorough knowledge and understanding of Scripture provided him the clarity and wisdom he needed to debunk the devil's lies and remain faithful to his Father.

Temptations come in many forms, and oftentimes we are unaware of these negative influences until it is already too late. A friend invites us to a bar to just hang out even though we have a final exam to study for. We drive the freeway and see the billboard advertising the strip club at the next exit. A coworker belittles us at a staff meeting, tempting us to return his condescension with a cutting remark. Temptations aren't always overt, and usually the most effective ones are subtle: "Can't you stay for just *one* drink?" Jesus, though, was so attuned to God's word and consequently, his voice, that even the subtle temptations were grossly apparent to him. "You are hungry. You have power. Why not use it to make bread out of these stones?" Doesn't seem like such a big deal. While many would be fooled by the devil's reasoning such as this, sacred Scripture revealed to Jesus what God was calling him to do and how he was to respond to those temptations.

Jesus shows us through his example how we, too, can combat daily temptations by taking time to read, pray, and reflect on God's word. Just like Christ, our knowledge of the Bible can help us to quickly identify negative influences in our lives and respond to them with poise and grace. In this way, we equip ourselves with all we need to keep the devil at bay and follow God's will in every decision we make.

God's Word Nourishes Our Soul

According to the Second Vatican Council's Dogmatic Constitution on Divine Revelation *(Dei Verbum),* sacred Scripture is the way which God cares for our soul. "For in the sacred books, the Father who is in heaven meets his children with great love and speaks with them; and the force and power in the word of God is so great that it stands as the support and energy of the Church, the strength of faith for her sons, the food of the soul, the pure and everlasting source of spiritual life" (*DV* 21). Through God's word, we are given all that we need to protect, edify, renew, and nurture our souls.

To keep her nuns vigilant against the beguiling traps of the devil, St. Teresa of Ávila offers a meditation based on Song of Songs 1:2, "Let him kiss me with kisses of his mouth." Teresa warns her nuns about how easily one's soul can be deceived through the false peace that the world, the flesh, and the devil offer. There are so many people who enjoy their surplus wealth, not realizing until it is too late that they have become enslaved by it. Their dependence and obsession with money leads them to hoard it for themselves, and they, in consequence, will be judged by God for every penny they spent frivolously, for they have forgotten that their wealth was not their own.

Teresa mentions that souls can also succumb to the false peace given through honors, as praise from others can quickly feed our pride and cause us to overlook the truth that God is the source of any virtue we possess. Our flesh is enticed by comforts and avoids suffering at all costs. This, though, goes contrary to the life of Christ who embraced suffering to the point of the cross. When we give in to the comforts the flesh desires, our soul weakens, and this is not the peace the bride desires.

The bride from Song of Songs, Teresa says, desires the peace that comes from perfect friendship with God. The bride passionately seeks union with the bridegroom, and Teresa understands that the only way to achieve this union is aligning our will with that of God's. Only then can our souls be at rest because it is through this eagerness to please and love him that we are given the courage to suffer in his name. Those who achieve this perfect union with God can be easily identified, because they no longer care for worldly affairs, riches, and honor. Their love for God is so strong that fear no longer controls them. Teresa writes, "Let us observe that when the soul begins to mortify itself, everything is painful to it. If it begins to give up comfort, it grieves; if it must give up honor, it feels torment; and if it must suffer an offensive word, the hurt becomes intolerable for it...But as it succeeds in its determination to die to the world, it will find itself freed of these sufferings...for the peace the bride asks for will have been attained."

Teresa prayed with the inspired word, allowing God to speak to her, and the result was this insightful meditation. Her example revealed how Scripture helps the soul see what it really needs. While the world fools souls with glimmer and gold, Scripture guides the soul to God, the only one who can truly give it the peace that it seeks. The souls of St. Teresa of Ávila and her nuns were nourished by God's word and through it, they learned how their souls were made to respond to the love of God.

God's Word Reminds Us of His Unfailing Love

"The Scripture passage that speaks to me the most is Matthew 18:12–14, when Jesus talks about the one lost sheep," Louis said during a youth ministry discussion I was leading.

"Oh? Can you tell us more about it?" I asked.

"Sure. Basically, Jesus tells his disciples a story about a

shepherd with a hundred sheep, and when one of them goes missing, the shepherd leaves the ninety-nine in search of the one that strayed," Louis continued. "The shepherd rejoices when he finally finds the missing sheep, and this, Jesus says, is how it is with God and us."

"Thanks, Louis. And what do you hear God saying to you through it?" I asked.

"Well..." Louis paused for a moment, seeming to search for the right words. "I'm adopted, and I never got a chance to know my biological parents." His brow furrows as his eyes dart to the floor. "I always felt abandoned by them. Don't get me wrong. My adoptive parents are incredible, and I love them so much. But I always wonder about my biological parents—who they are, what they were like, and why they decided to leave me."

The rest of the group was still while he spoke. I silently prayed: *God, please be with Louis. Give him healing and give him peace.*

"Whenever I read this Bible passage, though, I am reminded of how much God loves me," Louis said. "Through it, he tells me that no matter how lost or alone I feel, he will not abandon me. He will keep fighting for me. He will not rest until he finds me, because I am his." His eyes glimmered, and then he looked back at me.

"That is beautiful, Louis," I said. "Thank you so much for sharing how God spoke to you through this Scripture passage. Your faith is truly inspiring. Would anyone else like to share?"

Taylor spoke up: "Actually, I connect to that Scripture passage as well. I'm not adopted, and I can't imagine how you must feel." She gave a sympathetic glance at Louis. "But I struggle with my parents, too. They expect me to act and look a certain way, because in their eyes, I am a girl and girls should be girls. So, when they see me wearing basketball shorts and a cap to a family get-together or spending time playing hockey with the guys, they freak out. They can't seem to reconcile the fact that I am my own person, and because of it, I always feel like an outsider within my own family. Through this Bible passage, though, I hear God say to me that he will never give up on me, that he doesn't care about how I dress, and that all he desires is for me to come home and be with him. He loves me as I am."

Louis and Taylor heard God's loving voice through sacred Scripture. They identified with the one lost sheep and understood that God would never tire of seeking them out. Even though they may not have had the best relationship with their earthly fathers, Louis and Taylor had faith that their heavenly Father would never disappoint them, caring for them beyond all understanding.

God speaks directly to us through the inspired words of the Bible. God spoke to Jesus when he was tempted in the desert. He spoke to St. Teresa of Ávila and her nuns when they yearned to draw near to him, and he spoke to Louis and Taylor when they grieved over their complicated relationships with their parents. God, however, did not speak audible words to communicate with them. Instead, he used Scripture.

God's word has the power to console, guide, heal, pacify, elevate, and transform us. All we need to do is carve out moments throughout our day to pray, open the Bible, and listen to his voice. He yearns to spend time with you, and he has written words of great love to address every need you have. Whenever you read a passage in the Bible, ask yourself: *What does this verse or passage mean to me? Which person in the narrative do I most connect with? How does this story relate to my life? What is God trying to tell me through this Bible story?*

Allow his word to penetrate your heart and, soon enough, you will begin to better understand what his voice sounds like.

For Practice and Reflection

Here are two different ways of praying with the Bible. Use at least one of the following methods to experience God's voice through meditation over sacred Scripture:

Pray-as-You-Go podcast

1. Go to pray-as-you-go.org/home/ or search for another Bible meditation podcast online.

2. Click on the date you are reading this chapter.

3. Quiet your heart and begin with the Sign of the Cross. Ask God to help you hear his voice at this time.

4. Press "Play," close your eyes, and listen attentively to the podcast.

5. When the speaker asks meditative questions, respond to them mentally as if you were sharing your thoughts with the speaker directly.

6. While the passage is read again, think to yourself: *How might God be speaking to me through this Scripture passage?*

7. When the podcast ends, slowly open your eyes and thank God for the time you had to spend with him.

Lectio Divina

Here is a way of engaging in this prayer form which is relaxing and rather easy.

1. Select a passage from one of the Gospels in which Jesus is interacting with others.

2. Recall what you are doing in engaging with the word of God and what one desires from this encounter. God is present, and because God is present, one relies on God.

3. Read the Gospel passage twice so that the story and the details of the story become familiar.

4. Close your eyes and reconstruct the scene in your imagination. See what is going on and watch the men and women in the scene. What does Jesus look like? How do the others react to him? What are the people saying to one another? What emotions fill their words? Is Jesus touching someone? You may want to be in the scene, so place yourself in the scene, perhaps as an observer, as one lining up for healing, or as one helping others to Jesus.

5. Some people's imaginations are very active, so they construct a movie-like scenario with a Gospel passage. Others will enter the scene with verbal imagination, reflecting on the scene and mulling over the actions. Vividness is not a criterion for the effectiveness of this kind of prayer. Engagement is, and the result is a more interior knowledge of Jesus.

6. As you finish this time of prayer, you should take a moment to speak person-to-person with Christ, saying what comes from the heart.

≈

God speaks to us through sacred Scripture about many topics, including self-esteem struggles, dating concerns, and other areas of life. Has there been a time when God spoke to you through Scripture? What happened?

Jesus was able to effectively defend himself against the temptations of the devil because he knew Scripture inside and out. How familiar are you with Scripture? How might God be calling you to get to know him better through his word?

Louis and Taylor felt God's great love for them through Jesus's parable of the Lost Sheep. What Bible story or verse reminds you of God's loving presence in your life and why?

CHAPTER 5

God Speaks
through Silence

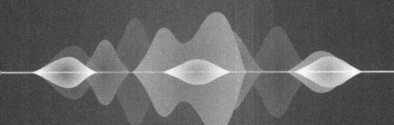

> "Our greatest need is to be silent before this great God with the appetite and with the tongue, for the only language he hears is the silent language of love."
>
> **ST. JOHN OF THE CROSS**

We hadn't seen each other for months. As I told her my latest news, my best friend received a text message—then another, and another. "This will only take a second, but keep going. I'm still listening," she said. And so, I continued. While she texted, I told her my struggles of the past few months balancing school and work. I confessed my deepest regret at not being able to spend more time with my grandmother before she passed away. Then, saving the best news for last, I expressed my immense joy in finally finding the person I felt God was calling me to be with. As I looked to her to celebrate, I suddenly realized she hadn't heard me. At all! Her eyes were still glued to her phone, she had no response to my happy news, and it was obvious that nothing I had said completely registered. I was initially fooled by her occasional nods and "uh-huhs," so it wasn't apparent that she hadn't been truly listening until I received her lackluster response to my exciting news. She had been physically present but mentally absent.

Have you ever tried to listen to your spouse, a friend, or a family member while watching TV? Typing an email? Listening to a ballgame or the news on the radio? How well were you able to listen?

While we may hear a few words here and there, we miss

subtle cues that add depth and meaning to what is being shared. When we look away to view the television screen, for instance, we fail to see the gloomy, downcast eyes of our friend as he says, "Yeah, I'm doing well. How about you?" When we continue typing as our spouse talks about his or her day, we thoughtlessly show through body language that what they have to say is not as important as the work we are doing. When we tune in to the radio while our supervisor tries to speak with us, our mental absence in those moments often results in misunderstandings. Consequently, listening requires all our faculties—our eyes, ears, mind, heart, and body.

This is especially true when we seek to hear God's voice. Just as we would give our full attention to our loved ones, we also are called to focus all our attention on God. Listening to God necessitates silence. This listening demands our presence—emotionally, physically, mentally, and spiritually. It begs for us to remove all distractions and invites us to step away from the noise emanating from our phones, TVs, computers, and the like. The silence required to hear God enables us to acknowledge his presence, reflect on his words, and reside in his love and peace.

Acknowledging His Presence

I gaze into her eyes as she gazes back into mine. I am filled with joy and purpose. I see nothing but her, and she sees nothing but me. All other thoughts fade. My precious baby girl—she alone consumes my attention. As I continue to gaze incredulously, I am reminded that she is mine and I am hers.

In this moment I become profoundly aware that this

must be a small taste of what God feels when he looks at us, his children. Just as I am enthralled by every little movement, hiccup, smile, and cry of my newborn daughter, God is engrossed by everything we do, think, or say. We captivate him. We pervade his thoughts because we are his. God gazes at us with great love and waits patiently for us to gaze back.

This is essentially what silence allows us to do—gaze back at God. When we quiet our hearts and minds, we permit ourselves to return the attentive love God continually gives us. When we are silent, we acknowledge God's presence, and we give him the opportunity to respond to our prayers. Silence is a posture of readiness and openness. It prepares us to listen to God's voice without judgment, fear, or pride. Silence reminds us that God is in our midst.

When we avoid moments of silence in prayer, we—in essence—close our ears to God. We tell him, "Sorry, but what I have to say is more important." This way of praying, however, is undoubtedly one-sided. We are speaking *at* God instead of speaking *with* him, causing us to miss all the glorious ways God may be trying to communicate with us. When we are with God, we should be like a baby with her mother—giving God all our attention and ready to respond to his every call by allowing moments of silence for him to speak.

How God Speaks through Silence

In 1 Kings 19:11–13, it is written, "There was a strong and violent wind rending the mountains and crushing rocks before the LORD—but the LORD was not in the wind...not in the earthquake...not in the fire; after the fire, a light silent sound...A voice said to him, Why are you here, Elijah?" Elijah expected God to speak through winds and earthquakes. This passage, however, reminds us that God often speaks to us in stillness and quiet rather than earth-shattering ways. It was through a "light silent sound" that God's voice was heard by Elijah, and had he not taken the time to sit in silence, he may have missed God's call entirely.

Mother Mary provides another great example of how silence allows us to hear God more clearly. During pivotal moments of her life, Mary spent quiet time alone to be with God and to listen to his voice. When the angel Gabriel appears to her with good tidings, proclaiming that she is favored by God, she silently "pondered what sort of greeting this might be" (Luke 1:29). Throughout our life, we will encounter messengers from God who deliver his truth to us, who challenge us to change our lifestyle, who support us during hardship, for example. It may be a sister, uncle, child, teacher, or even a stranger. Like Mary, we may not immediately understand the encounter or the message. The important thing, however, is to follow in her footsteps by taking the time to listen to the messengers God sends to us and quietly ponder everything that is said.

After the birth of Jesus, Mary and Joseph were visited by shepherds who proclaim amazing things about him: "And Mary kept all these things, reflecting on them in her heart" (Luke 2:19). Again, Mary wasted no time and silently pored over all that the shepherds had said about Jesus. How many times have we heard people speaking about God to us, and instead of prayerfully spending time reflecting on what was said, we hurriedly go on to finish another errand, turn on the television, check our social media accounts, and the like? When we hear about God—whether it is through the Mass, Scripture, a friend, or another source—the Holy Spirit invites us to take time to prayerfully reflect on the message. Ask yourself what the message means to you, how it relates to your own life, and what God may be telling you through it. This is what our Blessed Virgin Mary did. She pondered over every piece of news she heard about Christ, her precious Son, thinking about what it all meant for her, her family, and the world.

While all the disciples fled during Christ's passion, Mother Mary silently remained following behind him. "Standing by the cross of Jesus were his mother..." (John 19:25). Mary witnesses soldiers violently scourging, mocking, and spitting on her beloved Son. Even though she was stricken with sorrow, she did not try to stop it from happening. Rather, she faithfully followed her Son to the foot of the cross and solemnly embraced God's will. Silence often speaks more profoundly than words. Without any dialogue, Jesus knew the great sorrow his Mother was experiencing through her tears, and Mary knew the grave suffering her Son was experiencing through the blood he shed. Both were deeply aware of each other's loving and enduring presence.

Just as it was with Mary and Jesus, there are times when the Holy Spirit invites us to spend time in silence with God, to remain by his side, and listen to his voice. When my paternal grandmother passed away, I could not stop from crying. Wishing to be alone, I hiked up a mountain near my home. I found a large boulder away from the main trail to sit on, and it was there where I allowed all the tears to flow. In that time of grief and silence, I knew God was near. In the silence, he comforted me through the warmth of the sun. In the silence, he renewed me with the coolness of the wind, and in the silence, I sensed God saying: "You are not alone. This is not the end. You will see her again, and we will always be here for you. We love you."

Caution. Prayer Trap Ahead!
DISTRACTIONS

I try to pray as much as possible, but as soon as I begin, my thoughts start to wander. I remember the groceries I still need to add to my list, or the hurtful comment I received from my boss. Then just as my thoughts are winding down, I notice the beautiful dress of a woman who walked past my pew! How can I pray amid all these distractions?

Tip 1: Find a distraction-free refuge. What time and place works best for you to be with God? When do you have the house to yourself or when is the church a little less busy? What distracts you? Is it all the objects in your room, your phone, or the television? Finding the right time and being in an environment that is free of distractions will go a long way toward helping you focus on God. If the objects in your room distract you, turn the lights off and light a few candles instead. If you get easily distracted by other people, go to a quiet place where you can be alone. This is what Jesus often did (see Luke 5:16). If your phone is buzzing, the TV is blaring, or a staticky radio station is drawing your attention from God, turn them off. During times of prayer, set yourself up for success by putting all other people and distractions aside.

Tip 2: Refocus your thoughts with a word or phrase. If it is your own thoughts that distract you, call to mind a word or phrase that can refocus your thoughts. You can repeat the word "Jesus." Or you might mentally pray: *God be with me. Help me to be both physically and mentally present to you right now,* or anything similar. Any time you get a distracting thought, silently pray that word or phrase until the thought dissipates.

Tip 3: Offer your distractions to God. What thoughts are distracting you? If you have found a solitary and quiet place to pray but are still distracted, maybe your "distractions" are exactly what you are being called to offer to God in prayer. For example, perhaps you are kneeling at the foot of the cross at your church but you are thinking, *I can't believe my brother said that to me.* Try sharing with God what happened between you and your brother. He may be calling you to have patience with your brother and to forgive him. Sometimes our distractions are not distractions at all but are what the Holy Spirit is inspiring us to bring to prayer. Keep in mind that God wants to be part of your whole life, and this includes things that bother you.

A Great Need for Silence

Have you noticed how often we avoid quiet time? Many of us turn on the TV or radio as soon as we step into our homes or into our cars. When there is a lull in conversation, there is always someone in the room who feels compelled to break the uncomfortable silence. If we find ourselves alone, we immediately find something or someone to fill in the void.

I believe we struggle with silence because we fear the thoughts and feelings that may arise. Substances, for instance, are often used to numb feelings. Overwork and busyness are common tactics to avoid problems at home. Countless hours scrolling through social media accounts is our go-to when we're bored or in need of an escape. When we sit in silence, however, we become deeply aware of the stirrings of our heart—our hopes, frustrations, dreams, sorrows, and concerns. Running away from all that burdens us is no longer an option. Silence forces us to deal with our problems head on, and that can be a scary proposition indeed.

Silence amplifies our inner voice. It is the voice that tells us to skip the third drink or to help the homeless man on the road. This inner voice is the Holy Spirit, God dwelling inside of us. Yes, silence can be excruciatingly painful if we are not ready to face our problems. But silence is exactly what we need if we desire to hear God's voice. When we observe moments of silence in prayer, we begin noticing the pulls and pushes of the Holy Spirit. We begin to realize what God is calling us to do and what he is calling us to avoid. As such, silence attunes us to the workings of the Holy Spirit guiding us through the ups and downs of daily life.

Thomas Merton, a prolific Catholic writer, Trappist monk, theologian, and social activist, saw the great need for silence in our world and realized very early in his novitiate that God was speaking to him in the silence. "I am confronted with the fact of my past prayer," Merton wrote. "Acts, thoughts, desires, words, became inadequate when I was a novice. Resting in God, sleeping, so to speak, in his silence, remaining in his darkness, have fed me and made me grow for seven years."

Merton recognized that silence gave him what the world could not—peace. He was able to grow spiritually and enjoy the gift of God's tranquility. The silence urged him to keep his focus solely on God, and when he did, Merton was freed of all the worries that once burdened him.

Silence gave Merton true happiness. "If we strive to be happy by filling all the silences of life with sound, productive by turning all life's leisure into work, and real by turning all our being into doing, we will only succeed in producing a hell on earth," he said.

I find these words intriguing and quite relevant today because we often measure success and value in terms of productivity. Merton, however, understood the greater value of quiet and resting in God's love. Our desire to continually be "productive" can harm us if it is not balanced with moments of silence. And our ambitions can draw us away from God, especially if we allow them to control our actions, state of mind, and most of our precious time. Silence, though, compels us to prioritize the one and only thing that truly matters—God and our relationship with him. Yes, our jobs are important. Yes, household tasks need to get done. Yes, we are called to serve God by putting our faith into action by doing good works. But they all mean nothing if they are not centered in our relationship with God. Silence allows us to withdraw from the noise of our lives and enjoy the happiness that comes from remaining in God's great love for us.

Merton also believed that silence was the key to accepting oneself and others. "In silence we face and admit the gap between the depths of our being, which we consistently ignore, and the surface which is untrue to our own reality," he wrote. "We recognize the need to be at home with ourselves in order that we may go out to meet others, not just with a mask of affability, but with real commitment and authentic love."

Silence affords us the gift to earnestly know ourselves, and this self-reflection helps us to be more compassionate and merciful to others. For how can we reject the call to love others for who they are and as they are when, in silence, we come to know that we are loved for who we are and as we are by God? When we take time in silence to evaluate ourselves in light of God's perfection, we recognize just how far we have fallen and how much we are in need of his grace and mercy. Silence, then, helps us to become brutally self-aware, giving us the opportunity to address all the vices that keep us from God.

Silence not only prepares our mind, body, and spirit to hear God's voice, but it also gives us his peace, joy, and love. In the silence, we return the loving gaze of God. We say to him, "Speak, Lord, for your servant is listening!" (1 Samuel 3:10). In the silence, God's voice becomes clear. We hear of his great love for us. We hear his compassionate responses to our struggles, joys, frustrations, dreams, and all that is in our hearts. In the silence, we give God the opportunity to speak, and when he does, our very lives are transformed.

For Practice and Reflection

Two ways to experience hearing God's voice through silence are through:

Eucharistic Adoration

Eucharistic adoration is a Catholic tradition in which the consecrated host is adored by the faithful. Christ is truly present in the Eucharist, and we can be assured that he is with us whenever we adore him in this beautiful way. Most Catholic churches have scheduled times for adoration, so call your parish office or look at your church bulletin or website for more information. Here are some tips for eucharistic adoration:

- Set a realistic goal for how long you would like to spend in adoration. Start small, especially if you are not accustomed to praying in silence. Try ten minutes at first. Then increase it to fifteen minutes, twenty, and so on, depending on how the Holy Spirit is moving within you. Remember, it is not the length of time that matters but, rather, the quality of that time.

- Invoke the Holy Spirit during adoration and ask God to help you hear his voice.

- Gaze at the Blessed Sacrament and consider these questions: What would you like to say to God right now? What concerns do you have? What blessings are you thankful for? Who in your life needs prayer?

- Pay attention to the movement of the Spirit within you. What is the Holy Spirit inspiring you to do right now? Do you feel called to pray the rosary? Journal? Read a spiritual book? If so, then spend time doing just that.

- Then listen. What thoughts came to mind? What spoke to you when you prayed the rosary or journaled, for example? This may be exactly what God wants to share with you today.

- Close your prayer time with the Sign of the Cross.

Spending Time with God in Silence

When we spend time in silence, we give God the opportunity to speak. We, like Mary of Bethany, lay at the feet of Jesus, ready to listen to his voice. While Martha is "anxious and worried about many things" (Luke 10:41), Mary concerns herself with only one thing—being with Jesus. Our primary vocation beyond all others is to reside in God and in his love. Here are three tips for silent prayer:

- Find a quiet and secluded place—a park, your room, the church, or another peaceful place. It is essential that the location you choose is free of distractions and possible disturbances.

- Mentally share with God what has been on your heart and mind lately. Tell him all that is important to you as you would with your closest friend. If it helps, gaze at an icon, a painting of the Holy Family, or any other religious object that may help focus your thoughts on God.

- Allow thoughts stirring within you to rise to the surface. What came to mind as you pondered in silence? What passage of Scripture, words of wisdom, or other inspired memories made their way to your heart as you prayed? How does it all relate to what you just shared? What do you sense God is saying to you in response to your prayer?

∿

How easy or difficult is it for you to sit in silence?
What do you enjoy most about praying in quiet?
What are the obstacles you must overcome?

Have you ever sensed God speaking to you
while you were praying in silence?
If so, what happened and what did he say?

Elijah, Mother Mary, and Thomas Merton heard
God speak to them in the silence. Of these three
examples, whose story was the most intriguing?
Why?

CHAPTER 6

God Speaks through Tradition

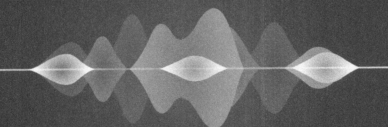

"You come to me and unite Yourself intimately to me under the form of nourishment. Your Blood now runs in mine, your soul, incarnate God, compenetrates mine, giving courage and support. What miracles! Who would have ever imagined such!"

ST. MAXIMILIAN KOLBE

Today is the day I will marry my best friend! As I walk down the aisle with my father sobbing beside me, I silently pray: *God, thank you so much for leading us to each other.* When I draw closer, I notice tears beginning to form in my beloved's eyes which, of course, spur tears of my own. We have gone through so much together, and I feel as if our tears were a joyous expression of all that we overcame to arrive at this moment. This is what I reflect on while we sing the "Gloria." Glory to God, indeed! He healed our once-wounded hearts so we could love each other as he intended. He is the reason for our joy and for the love we are celebrating now.

"In marriage you will find that it takes a lot of patience, humility, and mercy to keep the great love you have for one another alive," says the priest, beginning his homily. "But when you allow God to assume his rightful place at the center of your marriage, you can be sure that you will be given the grace needed to honor the vows you are making today." The word *grace* catches my attention. "Grace is favor, the free and undeserved help that God gives us to respond to his call" (*CCC* 1996). Before the wedding, I was anxious about whether I could be a good wife, and through the homily God responded to my fears saying: *Let go of any worry, for I will provide.* I am overcome with gratitude.

Next, our marriage vows: "I promise to be true to you in good times and in bad, in sickness and in health," says my beloved, looking at me tenderly. "I will love you and honor you all the days of my life." I revel at these words and how the beautiful sacrament of holy matrimony reflects what Christ does for his Church. My beloved and I are being called to give ourselves completely to one another, becoming vulnerable, and sacrificing our whole life for the betterment of each other. I silently pray: *God, help me to love my beloved as you love us—faithfully, fruitfully, freely, and completely.*

When it's time for the Liturgy of the Eucharist, I began missing my grandmother. I silently pray: *God, I wish Lola was here to celebrate this special day with us. I miss her so much.* I see the priest raise the host, and then hear God say to me, "But she *is* here, Carrell. When you receive me, you along with all the faithful here on earth and those departed are united. She is with you." The Eucharist *is* Christ, and there is no moment more powerful and more profound than consuming him on our tongues, in our bodies, and in our souls. I smile and begin imagining the communion of saints, angels, and my Lola around the altar, celebrating the selfless love and sacrifice of Jesus. What a sight to behold!

After Communion, my beloved and I walk toward the statue of Mary while "Ave Maria" is sung. We place flowers at her feet, kneel, and ask for her intercession. Mother Mary has been with us from the start. She interceded for us when our relationship was new and tenuous. I couldn't help but feel her warm embrace as we prayed. It was as if she was saying, *"I am so proud of you two for not giving up and for doing whatever my Son asks you."*

I hold her close in my thoughts and whisper, "Thank you," trusting she understands all that it meant. Finally, the priest gives a final blessing and exuberantly says, "Family and friends, I am happy to present the newly wedded couple in holy matrimony, AJ and Carrell!"

What Is Catholic Tradition?

Throughout our wedding ceremony, God and I were having an intimate conversation. Each part of the Mass was an opportunity for me to speak to him and for God to speak to me. Every prayer, song, Scripture passage, homily, and movement in the Mass offers everyone this same opportunity to encounter God.

God can speak to us not only in the Mass, but in every Tradition of the Catholic faith. Catholic Tradition is all the practices that have been given to us by our predecessors through apostolic succession. This includes all the prayers and teachings that unite us as Catholics. The Twelve Apostles were the closest friends and most devoted followers of Jesus. They walked, ate, laughed, cried, and suffered with him. It is through the apostles that the teachings, practices, prayers, and life of Christ has been passed down to us. As such, every teaching, prayer, and practice given to us from our first pope, St. Peter, to our current Holy Father, are ways in which God speaks to us.

The Mass is a celebration of God's love for us, his Church. The sacraments give us his grace to be made new in baptism, forgiven in reconciliation, nourished in the Eucharist, strengthened in confirmation, united in matrimony, ordained in holy orders, and healed in the anointing of the sick. Our *Catechism* says, "Christ now lives and acts in and with his Church...through the sacraments" (*CCC* 1076). Christ is truly present in every sacrament that is celebrated by the faithful. Through them, he gives us all we need to fulfill his call.

Traditional prayers enable Catholics worldwide to unite, expressing the same desire to worship, thank, adore, petition, and love God. All the other practices are simply different ways of helping us draw nearer to him. The Apostles' Creed, the rosary, our teachings on the communion of saints, Mother Mary, the Holy Trinity, and our practice of eucharistic adoration are other popular examples of Catholic Traditions. We can encounter God through any of these. Here are examples of people who have experienced this firsthand:

The Sacrament of Reconciliation

He came to me with tears streaming down his face. "Carrell, I haven't shared this with many people because I'm ashamed. I struggle with lust, and I find myself, uh [nervous pause], doing things I know aren't right. I want to overcome this, but I don't know where to start."

I waited for his eyes to meet mine and said, "Charlie, you have conquered half the battle already by admitting your faults and seeking help. Have you gone to confession yet?"

More tears streamed down his face as he said, "I feel so far away from God now. I guess...I'm afraid...afraid of what the priest will say, of feeling judged. I know I shouldn't be, but I am."

I nodded sympathetically. "You aren't alone in feeling this way," I said. "We all make mistakes we're ashamed of. But Charlie, nothing you do could ever make God love you any less. When you are ready, go to confession and ask the Holy Spirit to guide your confession. Then listen to what Christ tells you through the priest. Can you try that?"

Charlie nodded.

The next month, Charlie dropped by my office. "Carrell, I finally did it," he said. "While waiting for my turn, I asked the Holy Spirit to help me let go of my shame and fear, and to trust in God's mercy. The priest was very kind, and I didn't feel judged at all. He recommended that I attend an SA [Sexaholics Anonymous] recovery group and then, for penance, he asked me to reflect on the life of St. Augustine. And when the priest finally said, 'I absolve you of all your sins,' I actually felt that it was Christ who was speaking to me, telling me that he loved me and that I am forgiven. I feel so...so...free! Like this huge weight has been lifted off my shoulders. I just had to share my experience with you."

Caution. Prayer Trap Ahead!
SHAME

I've made so many wrong choices. I used drugs, hung out with the wrong crowd, and I can't seem to forgive myself. I feel lost. I can't talk to God anymore. How can I, with everything I've done?

Tip 1: Believe that nothing can make God love you any less. Like Charlie and this young soul, St. Peter the fisherman struggled with his own failings. After a hard night without catching any fish, Peter encounters Jesus, who tells him to cast his net again. Upon following his command, Peter's net is filled with so many fish that his boat nearly sinks. Peter, now aware that he is in the presence of God, falls to his knees and says, "Depart from me, Lord, for I am a sinful man" (Luke 5:8).

As we draw closer to God, perfect and holy, we become more aware of our imperfections and sinfulness. Peter felt he could not remain with Jesus because of everything he had done wrong. This, however, couldn't be further from the truth. Instead of leaving him in his despair, Jesus tells Peter and his friends, "Do not be afraid; from now on you will be catching men" (Luke 5:10). Jesus does not condemn them. Rather, he calls Peter and his friends to leave their pasts behind and follow him.

Isn't that what God calls us to do every time we make a mistake? To place our sins, darkest secrets, and most regrettable actions at his feet and then follow him in a life of truth, holiness, and love? Throughout the Bible, God continually shows his mercy towards those who ask for his forgiveness: the woman caught in adultery (see John 8:1–11), the corrupt tax collector (see Luke 19:1–10), and even those who were about to kill him (see Luke 23:34). Jesus' love for all these undeniably sinful people never changed. He was moved with compassion for them, and so it is with us. Nothing we do, no matter how grave, could make God love us any less.

Tip 2: Seek God's forgiveness. Jesus forgave and forgave and forgave. If someone was truly sorrowful for what he had done and sought to sin no more, God forgave him, even knowing that he might sin again in the future. Why? Because God does not expect perfection from us. He knows that we are human and will inevitably make mistakes. All he desires is that we keep running back to him like our courageous saints. They, too, were imperfect people. But what set them apart was that they continued to try. They strove for holiness, no matter how many times they failed, because they trusted in God's mercy and unconditional love.

Tip 3: Celebrate the sacrament of reconciliation. This sacrament is so powerful because it proclaims the words we most desperately need to hear in today's world:

"God, the Father of mercies, through the death and the resurrection of his Son, has reconciled the world to himself and sent the Holy Spirit among us for the forgiveness of sins; through the ministry of the Church may God give you pardon and peace, and I absolve you from your sins in the name of the Father, and of the Son and of the Holy Spirit" (*CCC* 1449).

So often, we are our own harshest critic. We condemn ourselves because we cannot look past our gravest mistakes. God knows our hearts and recognizes the agony we feel when we have done something wrong. Therefore, the sacrament of reconciliation is not for God's benefit but for ours. It is the way in which he provides healing for our souls. God forgives us through this sacrament and through the priest who is acting in the person of Christ. Furthermore, we are given the grace we need to strengthen our resolve from future temptations.

God wants to pour his love into your heart through the sacrament of reconciliation. He wants to shake your very being so you may learn the truth—you are forgiven, and you are his. Do not let your shame keep you from God. Instead, run to him and know that he will welcome you with open arms. You will find that, when you do, God is already waiting and joyfully preparing a banquet for you (see Luke 15:11–32).

The Rosary

Every night my grandmother would gather our family around the home altar, light candles, and lead us in the rosary. At the time, I thought, *Is this really what prayer is, repeating a bunch of words over and over again?* When my grandmother moved out of our home, though, my sister and I surprisingly began missing this time together.

Since we never led the rosary by ourselves, our mother offered us a booklet that laid out the instructions. I was fascinated with it, because it briefly described—and even gave an artistic rendering for—each mystery of the rosary.

When the third joyful mystery was read, I looked intently at the artwork. The barn seemed cramped. Here was the Holy Family surrounded and crowded by animals. It certainly was not the cleanest or most comfortable place to deliver a baby. The fruit of the mystery came to mind—poverty. As I reflected on this image, I was reminded how Jesus, the King of Kings, did not seek or expect riches and fame, even at his birth. Instead, he chose to live in poverty and in service to others.

It was here I realized that praying the rosary is like looking through your favorite photo album. As you point to a picture of your soccer team gleefully raising a trophy, you say to your brother, "Look. Remember this time when our team won our very first tournament?" Or, you say to your child as you show her a picture of you both arriving from the hospital, "Honey, see this? Look how small you were. Did you know that I spent eighteen hours in labor for you?" This is what we do when we pray the rosary. We relive, remember, and try to emulate all the pivotal moments of the life of Jesus and his mother, Mary.

While praying a particular decade, we reflect on a moment of their life and call to mind what God may be saying to us through it. An example of this can be seen through the story of Marsha. "Carrell, this month I felt like a complete wreck," she said. "My daughter seems to be ignoring my calls, my roof needs pricey work done, and my coworkers are driving me crazy. But then, I started praying the rosary and offering up all my resentments and worries to God. When I got to the second luminous mystery about the wedding at Cana, I couldn't help but think of how God even takes care of the things we may not think are very important. I mean, would it really have been the end of the world if the newlyweds ran out of wine at their reception? But still, Jesus turned the water into wine for them. I felt God say to me, '*You are going to be OK. I am here for you and will provide all that you need just as I did with the newlyweds.*' I felt a wave of peace wash over me, and I knew that everything would be all right."

The Saints

"To be honest, it's rather difficult for me to bear my sufferings patiently," my friend said to me. "When I lost my job, my first thought was: *Why, God? Why me?* Saint Maximilian Kolbe reminds me during these times that God can make something beautiful out of the messes of our lives if we allow it. Saint Max didn't let the evil surrounding him in Auschwitz overtake the love and faith he had in God. He clung to God and persevered through the most horrendous circumstances. When I go through a trial, I ask for St. Max's intercession, and I know that he and God will guide me through it."

"Saint Kateri Tekakwitha is one of my favorite saints," said one of my teens. "Saint Kateri had embarrassing scars all over her face, and she was looked down upon by her community for converting to Catholicism. Just like her, I often feel like the black sheep of my family. I am constantly picked on by my peers, and there are times when I feel like I don't belong anywhere. Saint Kateri, however, reminds me that I'm not alone. Whenever I ask for her intercession, she points out the people in my life who love me as I am."

"I absolutely love St. Faustina," a young adult proclaimed exuberantly. "I've read her diary, *Divine Mercy in My Soul*, and it's incredible. She talks about the conversations she has with God and the endless mercy Jesus has for us all. I pray the Chaplet of Divine Mercy daily, and she inspires me to do it. Through her, I learned the depth of God's forgiveness, and I am reminded in my daily life to forgive others as God has forgiven me."

These people heard God speak to them through our beloved saints. I like to envision saints as our cheerleaders in heaven who urge us on when we are losing hope and who, like Mother Mary, point us to Christ when we've lost our way. They are our heavenly friends who have fought the good fight, won, and like Christ, they give us an example to follow. Most important, our saints reveal the glory that comes when we say yes to God's will.

As with our saints, every Catholic Tradition is an opportunity to listen to God's voice. These Traditions are shared treasures from our departed brothers and sisters in Christ who found in them God himself. They are the known methods of communication to God. When you take part in any Catholic Tradition, mentally pray, *God, what is the meaning behind this Tradition and how are you responding to my prayers through it?* Soon, you also will experience the riches each Tradition brings.

For Practice and Reflection

Try any of the following to hear God's voice through our faith traditions:

The Holy Mass. When we fully participate in the Mass, we become more attuned to God's voice speaking to us.

- Arrive ten to fifteen minutes before Mass, grab a missalette, and reflect on that day's Scripture readings. Another option is to preview the readings at usccb.org/bible/readings. Reading the Scripture passages beforehand will allow his word to penetrate your heart, helping you to better receive his message.

- Before Mass, offer your intentions to God. Silently consider the concerns, struggles, blessings, or needs you want to share with him.

- Listen attentively throughout each part of the Mass. During each hymn, prayer, reading, homily, and rite, ask the Holy Spirit, *God, what are you trying to tell me through this?*

- When you leave Mass, ask God to help you remember and live out all you have heard and learned.

The rosary. Gently repeating the prayers of the rosary helps our hearts enter a restful silence, where God's spirit dwells.

- Visit rosary-center.org or buy a rosary pamphlet to learn this Scripture-based prayer.

- When you begin each decade, read and reflect on the specific mystery for that decade.

- While you say the prayers for each decade, ask yourself: *How does this moment in Jesus' or Mary's life relate to mine? What can I learn from their example? How is God speaking to me through the lives of Jesus and Mary?*

The Divine Mercy Chaplet. This is one of the many prayers to turn to when you need forgiveness or if you need God's help to forgive someone who has deeply hurt you.

- Visit thedivinemercy.org/message/devotions/chaplet or buy a Divine Mercy card to learn how to pray the chaplet.

- Begin this prayer by calling to mind who God is calling you to forgive. Is it yourself? Someone who has hurt you? A situation where you need healing?

- While you pray the Chaplet of Divine Mercy, reflect on the endless mercy God has for you. Ask him to help you extend his mercy to those you call to mind.

- Throughout the prayer, ask God silently: *What are you calling me to do regarding those who have deeply hurt me? How might you be calling me to forgive myself?*

The saints. Saints exist as role models, making it easier for us to imitate Christ. In other words, saints encourage more saints among us. Sanctity loves company.

- Read and reflect on the lives of the saints, either through books or by researching Catholic saints online.

- When you find a saint who interests you, ask God, *What can I learn from this saint, and what are you communicating to me through the story of his or her life?*

- Ask for the intercession of that saint. Remember, the saints are cheering you on from heaven.

~~~

Have you ever heard God's voice while you were at Mass? If so, what happened and what did you hear him say to you?

What Traditions of the Catholic faith are you most fond of and why? How does God speak to you through these Traditions?

Who is your favorite saint and why? How does this saint's life inspire you?

CHAPTER 7

God Speaks through Nontraditional Means

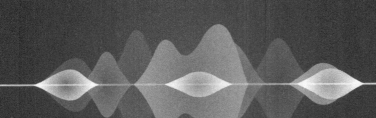

"Praised be you, my Lord, through Sister Moon and
the stars. In the heavens you have made them bright,
precious, and fair."

ST. FRANCIS OF ASSISI

I was having a particularly bad day. I was working at an afterschool program where I was assigned to work with fourth- and fifth-graders, an age group I wasn't very familiar with. It was rough. My disciplinary techniques that worked splendidly for my kindergartners and third-graders did nothing to quell this more rambunctious, talkative, and disruptive group. Feeling defeated and at a loss, I silently prayed: *God, I feel like I am being trampled on and I have no idea what to do. I tried to excite them with an activity but to no avail. Please be with me and this class.*

During their half-hour recess, I strategized for the next period—what I could do better, how I could make the lesson more interesting, and other techniques. As I continued to walk and monitor the grounds, one of my kindergartners interrupted my stride and muddled thoughts. With a huge grin on her face, she gleefully shouted, "Hi, Ms. C!"

I smiled and said just as loudly, "Why, hello there, Hailey!"

She proudly lifted her dainty arms, giving me a necklace of flowers. "Ms. C, this is for you!" she said. "I made it myself! Will you wear it?"

"This is so beautiful!" I replied with genuine amazement. "Thank you very much, Hailey. I love it!" As I lowered my head, she ornamented me with her garland of flowers, then skipped giddily back to her friends with her ponytail swaying.

In this moment, I understood that God was speaking to me. Although Hailey was unaware of it, Christ was acting in and through her. Hailey represented all the kindergartners and first-graders I had successfully learned to teach, care for, and even discipline. It took several months to finally feel competent with this age group. How could I have expected to take on older students without some trial and error—especially on my first day working with them? Her sweet smile and flower necklace were God's way of saying to me: *It's going to be OK. I'm here with you. See how appreciated you are? Take it easy on yourself and just do your best.*

What Are Nontraditional Means?

At the beginning of our walk with God, many of us make the mistake of figuratively putting him in a shoebox whose contents we "wear" only on Sundays. We only put on dress shoes for church because that's where they belong...where *God* belongs. This, however, couldn't be further from the truth. God is greater than a narrowly defined concept of him. He is not just the God of Sundays but the God of every day and of everyone. While silence, Scripture, and Tradition are how one would *most likely* hear God's voice, they are not the only ways God can speak to us.

Like my experience with Hailey, God can speak through other people. He can speak through a sunset. He can speak through a song, religious or secular. He can speak through the media—the news, TV shows, movies, and the like. He can speak through anything around us, as long as we pay attention and stay with him in prayer. I call these experiences "nontraditional" because they are often the unexpected ways God chooses to speak to us.

We know, for instance, that God can speak through dreams, because we have countless stories in the Bible that attest to this. In a dream, an angel tells Joseph not to be afraid of taking Mary as his wife (Matthew 1:20); the Lord appears to Solomon, telling him to ask for whatever he desires (1 Kings 3:5); and the wife of Pilate learns of Jesus' innocence (Matthew 27:19). We've heard of saints who experienced God speaking to them through visions (St. Catherine of Siena) and locutions (St. Teresa of Ávila). We are aware of those who sense God speaking to them through the seemingly ordinary moments of each day like St. Thérèse of Lisieux. We even know that Moses heard God speaking to him through a burning bush.

What makes these experiences nontraditional is that they are not the usual ways God speaks to us. While we can readily hear God's voice through Scripture and the homily at Mass, for instance, we would be understandably surprised to encounter God at the market or on our way to a party. As such, these nontraditional experiences are both unique and often inconsistent. They reflect the omnipresence of God who does not hesitate to meet us where we are and in a way that will reach us best. However, we must be keenly attuned to the workings of the Holy Spirit to notice them, and we have to have a strong understanding of sacred Scripture and Catholic Tradition to fully comprehend their meaning. Even so, these nontraditional means remind us that God is supreme. He can be found anywhere and in anything because he created it all.

We can find the Creator within his creation. God created the universe when it still had no form or shape. God created the light and the darkness. He created the oceans, skies, and the land. God created every kind of plant and animal. God created the stars and our two great lights, the sun and moon. He created the seasons, and he created time. God breathed life into man and formed woman out of his rib. God created everything above and below, and saw that it was good (Genesis 1:1–28).

Sometimes we lose touch of this truth about God, do we not? We go about our day seeing our classmates, coworkers, family, friends, and strangers without giving a second thought that they're all made in his image and likeness. We take a bite out of our scrumptious sandwich or a swig of cold water on a hot summer day, forgetting that it came from the ground he made and cultivated. We take a walk outside, wincing at the blinding brightness of the sun but not thanking the Creator who commanded it into existence. All these seemingly mundane moments, though, are opportunities to encounter God. Since he created it all, he can speak through it all. The following stories attest to this truth:

Dreams

"Carrell, you will never guess what happened—my aunt dreamed that I would be a missionary," Simon said as he came into my office. "I was so shocked because I had been praying about that exact calling. What is so fascinating is that this happens to her all the time. I believe God frequently speaks to her through her dreams, and I'm wondering if I am being called to mission work."

I beamed at him. "That is amazing. I'm so happy for you! Just remember, though, that God can call us to be a missionary in different ways. It could very much be that God is calling you to be a missionary in the traditional sense of going to foreign lands, proclaiming the Good News, and doing charitable work. Or it may mean that God is calling you to be a missionary right here and now in your school, at home, and in your work ministering to the teens."

Simon looked at me with wide-eyed wonder. "That's exactly what my mom told me. She said that I need to interpret my aunt's dream with caution, because the way in which God is calling me to be a missionary is yet to be revealed."

I smiled and said, "Your mom is very wise. Continue to ask God in prayer how he is calling you to be a missionary, and I'm sure you will know what to do next."

Dreams, like all the other nontraditional means, can often be confusing if they are not interpreted using quiet meditation and a firm knowledge of sacred Scripture and Tradition. As such, it's important to bring these experiences to God in prayer and reflect on whether they are in keeping with his word and Catholic Tradition. If they are, pay close attention to what God may be telling you through these experiences. If you are not sure, then you should discuss your dreams with a spiritual adviser.

Music

"Carrell, you sang so beautifully tonight," said Mary, one of my young adults, as I put away my guitar. "And that song, 'Waters,' gets me every time."

I blushed, saying, "Thank you. Yes, I love that song too."

Mary's eyes lit up. "Honestly, I've been going through a lot lately, and during adoration, I was telling God how much I needed him right now. When you sang 'Waters,' those lines: 'When storms surround me, you hold me close. When darkness overwhelms me, you light a path. God, your love will never fail me.' They spoke to me. I knew that God was with me telling me to let go of my fears, because if I keep my eyes on him, I will not fall."

I nodded. "I'm so sorry to hear that things haven't been going well. I'm glad you came tonight, and that God gave you comfort through the song. Just know that we are all here for you if you ever need us."

"Thank you," Mary said, coming forward to embrace me. "I really appreciate you saying that. I am slowly realizing that God has blessed me with all of you and that I need to put my pride aside and ask for help more often."

Circumstances

"My mom is a drug addict," Robert confided, looking downcast. We sat in silence for a few moments feeling the weight of these words. "It was hard growing up with a parent who was fine one moment and then angry the next. I felt like I was always on edge."

"I can only imagine how difficult it was to deal with her sudden changes in mood," I said.

"Yeah. Even now, after ten years of my mom being clean, I'm still struggling to forgive her and let go of everything I've gone through," Robert said. "All this time, I've been pushing these resentments aside, believing that if I just pushed them far enough, they would eventually go away."

"Forgiveness takes time. You can't help how you feel, and it's OK to struggle. Have you prayed about it?" I asked.

"That's the thing. I wasn't aware how deeply her addiction had affected me until I heard one of the conference speakers share his own struggle with drug addiction. I had to rush to the bathroom in the middle of the talk because I was afraid that I would just lose it in there. It hit too close to home." Robert quickly wiped a few tears from his eyes. "Then, a week later, as I was taking my morning run, I passed those DARE banners on the fence of the school next to my home. To top it all off, yesterday one of the segments on the radio show I listen to on my way to work was about addictions and how prevalent they are in America. After that, I just looked up and said: 'OK, OK, OK! I hear you, God, loud and clear!'" Robert said with a laugh.

"Wow, those were quite a lot of signs," I replied. "What did you feel God was trying to tell you?"

"Well, I felt that God was telling me that I needed to stop ignoring my feelings and actually deal with them," Robert replied. "Deal with what happened to me because of my mother's addiction. Deal with all the pain I've been carrying, and trust that God would eventually heal me from all of this."

"How beautiful that even when we are unaware of our needs, God helps us see what he sees and provides for us. How is God calling you to deal with your feelings?" I asked.

"I believe God is calling me to start going to therapy or maybe join a support group or maybe both," Robert said. "I just know that I need to seek help beyond myself if I truly want to heal from all of this. I am feeling much more hopeful. I know that with help, God will heal me."

Nature

Images of St. Francis of Assisi are fascinating. In many drawings, Francis is balding, unshaven, and barefoot. What is most curious, however, is what he is doing. He is often depicted surrounded by trees, birds, wolves, and other animals. They peer up at him while he preaches. Here is a saint who aligns himself with all of nature. He looks at ease among creatures, talking to them like he would with any of his human friends.

Francis saw God in all of creation—the sun, moon, stars, wind, air, water, fire, and even death—because he understood that God's hand was in it all. As a result, St. Francis respected, honored and praised everything, everyone, and every creature. He called all living things "brother" or "sister," because he knew that all of creation including himself was connected to one another through God who brought them all into being. "Keep a clear eye toward life's end," Francis proclaims. "Do not forget your purpose and destiny as God's creature." We are one of God's creatures, so Francis treated humans, animals, and all of nature equally, not elevating one over another.

God spoke to Francis through nature. Francis often prayed in solitude among the beauty of the woods, mountains, stars, and oceans, because these brought him closer to God. He discovered numerous spiritual lessons in nature, including how to battle with darkness. "A single sunbeam is enough to drive away many shadows," Francis said. He learned that if he clung to the light of Christ, no obstacle, no matter how grave, could overpower him. This example shows how Francis took time to apply what he observed in nature to the spiritual life, and as he did, he heard God's voice.

The Ordinary

Saint Thérèse of Lisieux is one of the most beloved saints and doctors of the Church. Her ability to express her intimate relationship with God in simple yet astounding ways was awe-inspiring. In her brief twenty-four years, Thérèse demonstrated how God can speak through ordinary things and people and how we can respond to his call by carrying out our everyday duties with great love.

Thérèse struggled with feeling small and weak in comparison to all the holy saints she had read about and admired. When she confided to God, doubting her ability to attain holiness, God spoke to her through an invention of her time—the elevator. Thérèse was entranced by it, seeing its function as analogous to the spiritual life. While we may feel trapped by our shame and weakness, Thérèse was quick to both admit her limitations and accept the mercy of God. She knew she was imperfect and would never get to heaven by her own accord. However, the saint we have come to know as the "Little Flower" desired to be with God and realized being little was a strength, not a weakness. Thérèse proclaims, "...the elevator that would lift me to heaven is your arms, O Lord!" God revealed to her he would give her the grace to attain holiness. He would lift her up. She just needed to keep God at the center of her life and ask to be carried.

When Thérèse asked God to help her see her place in the world, he spoke to her through the array of flowers in her convent's garden. "I had wondered...why all souls did not receive an equal amount of grace," she wrote. "I realized that if every tiny flower wanted to be a rose, spring would lose its loveliness and there would be no wildflowers to make the meadows gay." Although Thérèse had aspired to be great like a rose in a garden, she learned that each life has its role. In the eyes of God, no life is more important than another, and when we see each life as part of a larger whole, the sight or result is more beautiful than we could have imagined. Thérèse saw herself as part of a community within the body of Christ and understood she was valued and loved like all of the rest.

God also spoke to Thérèse through children. "It is to recognize our nothingness, to expect everything from God as a little child expects everything from its father," she wrote. Thérèse observed how children never hesitate to run to their parents for every need because they trusted their parents to provide out of love for them. She saw their dependence, trust, and love for their parents as a reflection of how our relationship with God was meant to be. As such, Thérèse received God's mercy and graces in abundance throughout her life because, to put it simply, she asked for it. She became a child, trusting in God's great love for her and accepting his forgiveness for all her failings.

Because of their openness and faith, Simon, Mary, Robert, St. Francis of Assisi, and St. Thérèse of Lisieux all heard God speak to them in nontraditional ways in response to their prayers. They recognized that God could speak beyond the walls of the Church, and they had sufficient knowledge and understanding of Tradition and sacred Scripture to ascertain what God was saying to them through these nontraditional means. They were able to hear his voice in unexpected ways, because they came to God with their needs and trusted that he would respond in a way that would reach them best.

For Practice and Reflection

To hear God's voice through nontraditional means, try these:

Music

1. Play a Christian radio station or stream Christian music.

2. For as long you like, close your eyes and listen carefully to the lyrics of several songs .

3. During each song, mentally ask: *God, what are you trying to tell me through this song? How does this song express the great love you have for me?*

4. If a song moves you, sing it aloud and offer it to God in prayer.

Note: God can speak to you through some secular songs as well, though the message may not be as clear.

Nature

1. Go to a quiet place outdoors. You could hike a trail, go to a park, or simply step out into your back yard.

2. Take a few deep breaths and observe everything around you—the rustling leaves, the birds soaring overhead, the sun's warmth on your cheek, or anything else that strikes you.

3. God created everything you see, hear, and touch. How do they reflect who God is?

4. Tell God what you find beautiful, any observations you made, or feelings that arose.

5. Then, ask God what he may be saying to you through these experiences. Often you will be amazed by how these insights can be ways God chooses to communicate to you about areas of your life.

Note: If you enjoy spending time outside, you might find it helpful to pray while taking a stroll through the park, for instance. Or try reading a saint's autobiography in your back yard. If being outdoors while you pray helps you draw closer to God, go for it.

Movies

1. While watching a film, reflect on the story, the themes, and the characters.

2. What speaks to you and why? Did you relate to any of the characters? If so, how does their situation relate to yours? What feelings or thoughts arose within you while watching this film? Share all of this with God.

3. Finally, ask the Holy Spirit to help you understand how God may be speaking to you through this film. Was there any part of the film that reminded you of God or something you read in Scripture? Did any of the characters inspire you?

Note: Not all films easily lend themselves to this process. However, the Daughters of St. Paul are adept at using and viewing media through the lens of the Catholic faith. You can find their spiritual reflections on specific movies on their website: media.pauline.org.

News

1. Invoke the Holy Spirit, asking God to help you see the news through his eyes.

2. Watch or listen to the news over several days.

3. Reflect on the feelings and thoughts that stir in you and share this with God. In prayer, think about the following: *What piece of news troubled me? What news gave me hope? Where did I see the hand of God in the news I heard? Who or what am I being called to pray for after following the news?*

4. When you are finished, spend some time in silence to listen to what God has to say to you through the news you just experienced.

≈

In this chapter are six different examples of people who experienced hearing God's voice through nontraditional means: people, dreams, music, circumstances, nature, and the ordinary. Of these, which account intrigued you most and why?

Have you ever experienced God speaking to you in a way you did not expect? If so, what happened?

This book explains that God can speak through anything and anyone. How can you best prepare yourself to hear God's voice throughout each day?

CHAPTER 8

Discerning
God's Will

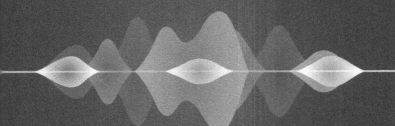

"For I know well the plans I have in mind for you—oracle of the LORD—plans for your welfare and not for woe, so as to give you a future of hope."

JEREMIAH 29:11

Several years ago, my husband and I were graced with the most amazing and—at the time—alarming news. A baby was on the way! I realized then I had a major decision to make: remain working full time as the director of youth and young-adult ministry or stay at home to care for our newborn. It was a difficult time of discernment because each choice had its share of heartbreak—both paths leading to my inevitable separation from those I've been blessed to care for. *What was I to do?*

As soon as the thought entered my mind, I knew I had asked the wrong question. The right ones were: *What was God calling me to do? Who knows better which path is best if not the One who sets us on it to begin with?* God called me six years ago to conquer my fears of failure and inadequacy and to become the youth minister he needed me to be. Likewise, it had to be God to tell me when I had fulfilled this important mission. I offered him my question of discernment and was met with silence.

Silence from God can often be mistaken for "no one is listening," but with God, this is never the case. He loves us. He calls us by name (see Isaiah 43:1). He knows "even the hairs of your head" (Luke 12:7). Sometimes God's silence means the exact opposite of not listening. He is silent to give us the freedom to vent, ponder, or express whatever we are feeling and thinking.

During this time of silence, I was being drawn to reflect on the years I had served as a youth minister—the ebbs and flow of ministry, the joys and frustrations, my favorite and worst moments—all replaying themselves in a mental three-hour movie. Then, I was driven to reflect on these words: parent, mother, baby, and "The Domestic Church" (*CCC* 1655–58). These words were imbued with meaning, purpose, and another mission of its own—to nourish the life growing physically, emotionally, and spiritually within me. After seeing the potential fruit in both, my next question to God was, *"Well, can't I do both?"*

This time, he spoke. Not in a booming voice from the clouds, like an angel, or with an ethereal vision. I'm sure any of these would have rendered me unconscious, so much so that I wouldn't have heard his message. Instead, he spoke ever so gently, urging me to see what was in front of me. As I carried this prayer in my heart, I began seeing. First, it was my ministry calendar. I counted the months and realized my baby would be born in October, my busiest time due to all our fundraisers, retreats, and other events.

Next, it was my daily ministry schedule. I work at least three weeknights, most weekends, and more hours than my job description specifies. This is typical for most ministers I know, and although I hadn't really minded it, I sensed that God was asking me: "Will you mind it when you've only gotten two hours of sleep the night before and then have to go to work to bring a youth group to another event?"

Then, God spoke through people I encountered. As people enthusiastically inquired how I was feeling and what I was planning to do, many responded with inspired words. His face and his words were revealed in theirs.

"If I had to do it all over again, I would have stayed home and learned to live with less," a mother of two told me. "I felt like I couldn't adequately do both."

"So many parents work instead of choosing to stay home because they have to," a married young adult said. "They wouldn't be able to afford staying home with their child. If we could afford it, I would stay at home, because there are so many children who would benefit from a parent who is continuously present for them."

"When you have that baby, you begin realizing that they are the priority," many mothers and fathers told me. "Everything else comes second." As I pondered those words, once again the Holy Spirit urged me to see what I had already begun seeing—a new mission on the horizon.

Last, God reminded me of the ministry I am most passionate about—spiritual direction. The daily grind of youth ministry often prevented me from giving the spiritual direction ministry he has blessed me with adequate time to develop and grow. Staying at home for at least a year would allow me to accept more speaking, spiritual direction, writing, worship leadership, and retreat direction opportunities, all of which would build up this ministry.

Two months after we received the pivotal news, I discerned that God was calling me to leave my position. He listened, spoke, and revealed his plans for me. I even felt his warm embrace through the farewell parties held in my honor.

Defining Discernment

Discernment is a process of uncovering God's will about a significant decision in our life. Discernment allows God to assume his rightful place at center stage and, in effect, choosing to say yes to his call. We turn our ears toward those around us, receive advice from others, and pay close attention to the stirrings of our heart. We pore over Scripture searching for answers. We listen closely at Mass, expecting God to speak. Like a sponge, we absorb every bit of wisdom that comes to us, comparing it with what we hear in Scripture and Catholic Tradition. In silence, we listen closely to where the Holy Spirit is leading us.

This process of discernment, however, can be difficult and overwhelming when we aren't accustomed to the way God speaks. My directees often ask:

- *Instead of truly listening and hearing God's voice, how can I be sure that I'm not just hearing what I want to hear?*

- *There are times when I find myself stuck between two choices. When I pray, I can find reasons God would call me to pursue either option. What should I do when I find myself in this situation?*

- *I am confused. Every time I pray about which decision to make, I hear too many voices in my head. Help!*

These questions reflect my directees' yearning to do God's will. They are actively seeking his voice, but in their search, they find it increasingly difficult to hear him amid all the noise. The opinions of others begin to confuse them. Their thoughts are scattered, and soon, even reading from Scripture becomes indecipherable. When you find yourself in this predicament, it is helpful to put into practice everything you learned from the previous chapters.

Tips for Discernment

Tip 1: Spend Time in Sacred Silence. Reading through the Book of Psalms is like listening to a private conversation among friends. It is raw with emotion. It bleeds vulnerability and brims with complete trust and acceptance. It is an intimate pouring out of the heart from the psalmist to God, holding nothing back and radiating great faith. The psalmists took time in silence to be with God and share the deepest parts of themselves with him.

In Psalm 25:2, for example, the psalmist writes, "Do not let me be disgraced; / do not let my enemies gloat over me." The psalmist admits to God his fear of enemies triumphing over him and expresses his desire to be vindicated. Then, he asks God to help him live righteously. He prays, "Make known to me your ways, LORD; / teach me your paths. / Guide me by your fidelity and teach me, / for you are God my savior" (Psalm 25:4-5). The psalmist came to God with all his concerns and needs, firmly believing God would direct his every step.

In this way, God invites us in silence to come to him and ponder the weight of the difficult choices we must make.

Silence enables us to confront the inner stirrings of our hearts. It helps us discern our deepest thoughts, feelings, and hopes. When we are silent, we give the Holy Spirit time to work his way from our thoughts and into our hearts, guiding us to the path where God resides.

If we truly wish to discern God's call, we must first take the time to be with him, like the psalmist, openly sharing our doubts and desires. During these ambiguous and confusing moments in our lives, Jesus asks us what he had asked the first disciples: "What are you looking for?" (John 1:38). In other words, what are you seeking? What question is weighing on your heart that you feel God is calling you to discern? Break away from all the noise that clutters your life and have a heart-to-heart conversation with God, who desires to walk beside you through it all.

Tip 2: Seek Wisdom. Rose and I met for spiritual direction because she was struggling to understand God's will regarding her love life. Sam, the man she was dating, was pressuring her to do things against her values. As she prayed for guidance, she read 1 Corinthians 13:4: "Love is patient, love is kind…it does not seek its own interests, it is not quick-tempered." She mulled over this verse, wondering if the relationship she was in reflected this unconditional love. Then she felt called to read St. John Paul II's *Theology of the Body*. As she searched for answers, God's voice became clear. Although Sam was kind and respectful at the beginning of the relationship, this was no longer the case six months later. Rose realized that, as much as she loved him, God was telling her to move on.

We can learn from the way Rose discerned God's will for her relationship with Sam. While we may ruminate over significant decisions incessantly in our minds, relying solely on our knowledge and experience, Rose quickly admitted her limitations. Her humility thrust her into action. She consulted sources and expanded her knowledge of the situation. She sought spiritual direction. She looked to Scripture and pored over the writings of St. John Paul II. In the same way, we can better understand which choice to pursue when we humbly seek wisdom from the spiritual wealth of our Catholic faith. Among the best sources to consult during your time of discernment include:

- Scripture—If you are having difficulty understanding or differentiating God's voice among your own and that of others, first read and reflect on the life, teachings, death, and resurrection of Christ in the Gospels. Becoming familiar with his voice in Scripture will bring clarity regarding your decision. What does Scripture have to say regarding your decision? How is God speaking to you through the Bible? What path most reflects the values and teachings of Christ?

- Tradition—When we are trying to uncover God's will, our Catholic Traditions offer great insight. Many of our saints have asked the same questions, so reading and pondering how they approached similar situations can be fruitful. Participating in the Mass fills us with the grace we need, giving us the courage and perseverance to follow his call. Oftentimes, the homily, readings, or prayers can be ways God speaks directly to us in response to our question. Research papal encyclicals, frequently celebrate the sacraments, and look for prayers and saints who relate to your decision. How is God speaking to you through these Catholic Traditions about the paths you must choose?

- Nature—In his book *Discernment*, theologian Henri Nouwen writes: "God's first language is nature," because it "points to God and offers signs and wonders indicating God's presence and will." By observing and contemplating God's glorious creation, we become more aware and appreciative of the natural beginning and end of all things. We see that growth requires continual nourishment and pruning. We come to realize that the death of plants and animals give way to the creation of new life, and so it is with us. We are continually being called to die to certain aspects of ourselves to bring about the growth and healing God desires for us. When you spend time observing God's creation, what "signs and wonders" speak to you? How do aspects like the cycle of life relate to you and the decision you must make?

- People—God places people in our lives for a reason. Pay attention to inspired encounters with friends, family, religious leaders, and even strangers. If asked, they will share their own experiences or offer words that may resonate with your area of discernment. The advice and experiences shared by wise mothers, fathers, and young adults were inspiring, because it clarified where I felt God was leading me. How has God spoken to you through others about the decision you need to make?

- Nontraditional Means—When we are open to hearing God's voice and actively seek him, he can speak through anything and anyone, including a song on the radio during your commute to work, a story in the news during your lunch break, a piece of artwork you spot during your morning run, and more. These can be opportunities for God to speak to you. Has God spoken to you about your decision in unexpected ways? What did you sense him saying?

Tip 3: Listen to Your Heart. There are times when the wisdoms we have gathered conflict with one another. What would I have done if one mother said to me that she hated staying at home and another shared the exact opposite? In cases like these, take everything that you learned about your specific situation and listen closely to your heart. It can offer you the guidance you need to understand what God may be calling you to do.

What does your heart say to you? What are your passions, hopes, and dreams? Which decision best aligns with these desires and the values of our beloved faith? What doors have been opened and which have closed? What brings you joy? What choice would embitter you? We can gain perspective on our discernment questions by delving into what lies at the core of our souls. Reflect on the various aspects of the choices you are considering and pray about which choice is in keeping with where your heart is leading you.

Tip 4: Test the Call. Henri Nouwen felt a strong pull to live and serve the poor in Latin America. However, he was a respected professor at Yale Divinity School and understood that choosing to pursue this opportunity would mean having to leave all he knew behind. After a long period of discernment, Nouwen finally decided to test the call and leave Yale. "Sometimes the way to know where you are called to be is to go where you feel you need to go and be present in that place," Nouwen wrote. "Soon you will know if that place is where God wants you." He hoped that once he tried living that calling, Nouwen would know with certainty whether God was truly leading him to serve the poor in Peru. This is exactly what happened. Although he felt an intimate connection with the country, Henri discovered that he was not meant to live among the poor. He was not accustomed to the harsh conditions they continually suffered and, in time, Nouwen felt that God desired him to use his gifts elsewhere.

Just as Nouwen courageously tested the call to determine its authenticity, so should we have the courage to test ours. After spending time in fervent prayer, seeking wisdom, and listening closely to your heart, we must take a leap of faith and live out the call. Is it what you expected? Is it not? As much as it pains us to find out, this test brings us closer to understanding where God is truly leading us.

Tip 5: Choose Love. Finally, pray about which choice would enable you to love God and others more fully. Two verses that readily come to mind during times of discernment are 1 Corinthians 13:1, "If I speak in human and angelic tongues but do not have love, I am a resounding gong or a clashing cymbal," and John 15:13, "No one has greater love than this, to lay down one's life for one's friends." We can be the most moving orator, successful businessperson, famed writer, esteemed professor, inspiring minister, or skillful doctor, but without love for God and others, we have nothing. When we finally meet God face to face, he will not ask us what type of car we drove, how much money we made or donated, how admired or successful we were, or even how many good deeds we did on earth. Instead, God will ask us only one question: How well did you love me and your neighbors?

The life of Jesus was one selflessly lived for God and for others. Jesus, both man and God, poured his heart out to serve those in need and, when the time came, he willingly suffered a violent death to save them. Love embraces the cross of suffering. Following Jesus' lead, all of our beloved saints have continued his ministry of service and doing everything with great love. Catherine of Siena heard God tell her to serve the poor and sick, and so she visited them in their homes and at hospitals. Thomas Aquinas glorified God through his writings, which have brought countless souls to a deeper understanding of God and the Catholic faith. Saint Stephen was the first to be martyred for boldly proclaiming the gospel. Padre Pio received the painful gift of the stigmata and was known for his humility, piety, and extraordinary spiritual charisms. While dying, Maria Goretti forgave the man who violently murdered her. These saints, and countless others, demonstrated their love of God and others through their service, mercy, and sacrifice. They loved God so much that they followed him to the cross, accepting their suffering with joy and purpose.

If you are still struggling with the decision you are discerning, consider: Which decision brings out the best in you and in others? Which choice enables you to draw closer to God? Which path would enable you to love God and others more completely? Generally, the choice that brings you closer to God and allows you to give of yourself and to others with selfless love is exactly where you need to be.

For Practice and Reflection

Entrust your life to God, and he will guide you. Try these steps to help you discern God's will in prayer:

1. Share with God the decision you are struggling with.

2. Reflect on all the wisdom you have gathered regarding the decision you need to make.

3. Make a list of the advantages and disadvantages of the choices before you, drawing upon Scripture verses, traditional Catholic practices, and the experiences of others that relate to each choice.

4. Spend time in adoration or a solitary place and bring this list to God. Ask him to help you be aware of any biases that you may have regarding the choices.

5. Amend your list as you begin receiving more insights during prayer.

6. Continue to bring this decision to God in prayer, until you sense God calling you to make a specific choice.

7. Close each prayer session asking God to help you seek his will above all else. You may use this discernment prayer:

Prayer for Discernment

God, right now I feel incredibly lost and confused. There are so many paths to choose from, and I just don't know which one to take.

Give me wisdom to understand which path is the one that will lead me closer to you.

Teach me humility so that I choose the path that allows me to love you and my neighbor more completely.

Grant me patience to allow your will for my life to unfold.

Open my eyes so that I can view each choice objectively.

Prevent me from being tempted to make the choice that may give me momentary happiness instead of the lasting joy and peace that comes from doing your will.

Help me to trust that you have a glorious plan for my life— much better than my own.

God, I seek to do your will above all else. I place this decision in your hands with confidence and faith that you know what is best for me. I offer my life to you. Amen.

〰️

What are you currently discerning? Has God
spoken to you regarding this decision yet?

What do you normally do when you are discerning
something of great importance in your life?
How is your process similar or different to what
is described in the "Tips for Discernment"
section of this chapter?

Which tip do you need to spend more time on?
How will this tip help you better understand God's
will regarding the decision you need to make?

CHAPTER 9

Let the Life-Changing Conversation Begin!

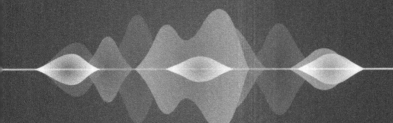

"Prayer is...being on terms of friendship with God, frequently conversing in secret with him who, we know, loves us."

ST. TERESA OF ÁVILA

C hrist's appearance to two of his disciples on the road to Emmaus (see Luke 24:13–35) is a reminder of how our doubts, fears, anguish, and egotism often blind us from seeing God. These two disciples had spent ample time following Jesus as he performed miracles, preached throughout the land, healed the sick, and pardoned contrite hearts. Yet when the resurrected Jesus stands face to face with them, they do not recognize him.

We read that when Jesus approaches and asks them what they are discussing, the two disciples mistake him as a stranger and look "downcast" (Luke 24:17). As the disciples recount the death of Jesus to the stranger, it becomes apparent that they didn't fully understand all that transpired. The disciples had expected Jesus to redeem Israel in triumphant glory. They didn't expect to witness their Redeemer being humiliated, beaten, and hung on a cross. They didn't expect Jesus, the miraculous healer, to bleed. They didn't expect Jesus, the inspiring preacher, to fall silent at the hands of his persecutors. In consequence, doubts began flooding their minds: *Maybe Jesus wasn't the Redeemer after all.*

Jesus appears to us each day, but how often do we notice him? How often are we so distracted by our problems that we fail to see his enduring presence in our lives? Like the disciples, our brokenness and despair can prevent us from hearing

God. He can address the struggles we bring to him in prayer, but if we continue to dwell in our pain, we will miss out on all the ways God is trying to repair our hearts and transform our suffering.

Our expectations of how our prayers should be answered and what our relationship with God should look like can also become an obstacle to drawing closer to him. The disciples began doubting Jesus as the true redeemer of Israel because they expected him to redeem the world through military conquest—not through his own death. God's plans, however, are far superior to our own. He says, "For as the heavens are higher than the earth, / so are my ways higher than your ways, / my thoughts higher than your thoughts" (Isaiah 55:9). Our faith, then, must exceed our human expectations of what "should" be. Our faith must cling to the truth written in our hearts: God is our good Father who redeems us through the blood of his only Son, Jesus Christ, because he loves us more than we can ever possibly imagine.

God's Love Is Triumphant

When we suffer, it may be difficult for us to trust in God's plan for our lives. We may become so despondent that we forget God can not only heal our pain, he can transform it. This, however, only exacerbates our suffering, because when we focus our attention on the darkness that surrounds us, we forget about the One who wishes to liberate, rescue, and guide us out of it. We, in effect, become the two disciples who are no longer able to recognize the face of God before them.

Nonetheless, had the disciples not first shared their disappointment with Jesus when he approached them, they never would have received the response they needed to look past their pain and celebrate the victory of Christ's death and resurrection. In this same way, we are called to share with God our deepest pains and greatest disappointments—even if they are about him. The two disciples did not keep their despair hidden. Instead, they offered it to Christ who in turn, helped them to understand that the suffering he faced was the way God redeemed the world.

More significantly, Jesus' life, death, and resurrection show us that God has the power to make "all things work for good for those who love God, who are called according to his purpose" (Romans 8:28). His death was the embodiment of faithful obedience, perfect love, and endless mercy. Jesus trusted and obeyed God's will even when it meant that he must suffer. He sacrificed his own life so that we, his Church and his body, might live and know what love truly looked like—a gift of self to others. Jesus revealed the depth of God's mercy by willingly receiving the just punishment meant for us and, in doing so, he redeemed the world.

God's love triumphs. Jesus conquered death with his resurrection, defeating evil with selfless compassion. Christ's suffering was transformed in a way no one thought possible. His death became the sign of victory for all who believed in him. Jesus can turn our sorrow into joy, our heartache into peace, our anger into mercy, our pride into humility and—like Christ and his crucifixion—our suffering into glory. God can breathe life into any hopeless situation that we entrust to him. Jesus' resurrection was proof that God triumphs over all evil and suffering. He fought and won the battle then. Will he not also fight and win yours today?

More on the Inner Voice: the Holy Spirit

When we are unaware of God's presence, silence helps us listen to the Holy Spirit. The two disciples, for example, could sense that the stranger was sharing something of great importance to them: "Then they said to each other, 'Were not our hearts burning [within us] while he spoke to us on the way and opened the scriptures to us?'" (Luke 24:32).

Is this not how it is with us when we silently ponder difficult decisions? Something within us tugs at our heartstrings and pulls us in one direction. When we are about to do something wrong, that inner voice compels us to reconsider. When we hear or read something profound, that inner voice encourages us to listen closely. When we have lost our way, that inner voice guides us back to where God lives.

That inner voice burning within us is the Holy Spirit, seeking to lead us to God. Whether we recognize it or not, the Holy Spirit urges us to see the face of Christ in our midst. By being silent, the Holy Spirit was able to work within the two disciples, helping them listen to and understand the stranger as he explained the Scriptures and all that had happened to Jesus. Just so, if we wish to draw closer to God and understand his plan for our life, then we must pay close attention to the Holy Spirit by remaining silent when he speaks.

Tradition Unveils God's Presence

It is in the breaking of the bread that the two disciples finally realized that the individual was no stranger but the resurrected Christ. Through this tradition, the disciples remembered how Jesus broke bread with them while he was still living.

"While he was with them at table, he took bread, said the blessing, broke it, and gave it to them. With that their eyes were opened and they recognized him, but he vanished from their sight" (Luke 24:30–31).

As with the disciples, our ability to see God at work in our everyday lives is greatly enhanced the more we celebrate his loving sacrifice through the Mass. We hear his voice through the Liturgy of the Word and are united to him through the Liturgy of the Eucharist. Jesus works through the sacraments, and these sacraments nourish, renew, fortify, pardon, unite, and heal us. Most of all, they are visible signs that reveal Christ's presence in our lives.

By interpreting Scripture and breaking bread with the disciples, Jesus revealed his identity to them. Similarly, when we struggle to see God at work in our lives, celebrating the Traditions of the Catholic faith can unveil God's hidden presence with us. Through these Traditions, especially the Eucharist, Jesus Christ says to us all: *Here I am. Consume me, and I will continue to live in you always. I will nourish you for the journey ahead. I will give you my strength, my peace, myself.*

The Importance of Community

The two disciples understood the importance of community. Once they realized they had been speaking to the risen Christ, they "set out at once and returned to Jerusalem where they found gathered together the eleven and those with them who were saying, 'The Lord has truly been raised and has appeared to Simon!'" (Luke 24:33–34). By seeking out their community, they found they were not the only ones who had witnessed the mystery of Christ's resurrection.

Like the apostles, our brothers and sisters in Christ are here to support us in our journey to heaven. They offer their own experiences of God that can strengthen, affirm, and encourage us. Our faith community reminds us that we aren't alone in this seemingly uphill struggle toward God. Our spiritual friends hold us accountable when we are tempted to go astray. They help us to remember God's promises when we have lost hope. They convey the wisdom they have received through their own failings and successes, and as a result, they give us a better chance at becoming the saint God calls each of us to be.

Furthermore, God continually calls us to pray as a community and for our community: "For where two or three are gathered together in my name, there am I in the midst of them" (Matthew 18:20). The Catholic Mass, rosary, and Creed are examples of communal prayers that unite us to the body of Christ, the universal Church. Our communal prayers remind us of the Trinitarian relationship of God who is a communion of three divine persons—the Father, Son, and Holy Spirit. Our prayer life, then, cannot exist in a bubble. Just as it is with our triune God, we also are called to be in communion with others. We pray with each other, reciting common prayers to bring glory to God with one uniting voice, and we pray for each other, including the needs of our fellow Catholics as well as those all over the world.

"In Christian prayer, no one asks for bread for himself: he pleads for it for all the poor of the world," Pope Francis says. Has someone close to you died? Pray not only for the repose of the soul of your loved one, but also for the souls of all those who have died unexpectedly. In this way, we conform ourselves to Christ, who unceasingly advocated and sacrificed on behalf of others.

Finally, our community takes us further in our faith than we could ever reach on our own. So, surround yourself with fellow Christians. Join a Bible-study group, young-adult group, prayer group, or any small faith community so you can learn from each other. Most importantly, actively participate in the holy Mass every Sunday, as it is your opportunity to pray alongside your brothers and sisters in Christ.

Caution. Prayer Trap Ahead!
BOREDOM

I hate to admit this, but I find prayer boring. I want to be closer to God, but I can't seem to make myself want to pray. Help!

Tip 1: Reflect on how you would like to pray. Those bored in prayer often have lost interest in the *way* they spend time with God. You can pray in almost any way that interests you. If you like being outside, take your Bible and read God's word there. If you enjoy walks, pray the rosary while you stroll alongside a lake. If you love art, pray while you paint a portrait of Jesus. Again, prayer is a living, personal relationship with God. Just as you would spend time doing different things with your best friend, you are not limited in the ways you choose to spend time with God. In short, think about what you already enjoy doing and invite God to come along.

Tip 2: Remember that relationships take effort, compromise, commitment, and patience. Think about the people who are most important to you. Can you think of a time when you didn't feel like being with them? Why? Let's face it, even in our most cherished relationships, there are times when we don't *feel* like being with our loved ones. Maybe we are angry or disappointed with them.

When we love someone, however, we show it by remaining by their side not only during good times but also, the bad. We demonstrate how important they are in our lives by working through any difficulties that arise in our relationship. We share with them what made us angry so they have an opportunity to apologize and change. We listen to their grievances about our own behavior because we love them and wish to make them happy. We go and watch a movie of their choice because they have already indulged us by watching ours.

In a similar way, our relationship with God can't always be about me, myself, and I. There are times when God calls us to spend alone time with him in silence, because he needs our undivided attention. God asks us to attend Mass, for instance, on the Lord's day because this is where he offers himself to us in the Eucharist. Yes, prayer can be enjoyable if we allow God to take part in what we most enjoy doing, but if we want our relationship with him to grow, we must also make a commitment to spend time with him in ways he calls us—even when we don't feel like it.

Tip 3: The more time you spend with God, the more you will want to be with him. If you are new to prayer, start small. Nothing is more self-defeating than setting unrealistic, overly ambitious goals and expecting yourself to reach them within that same week or even that same year. Begin with an allotted amount of time that you are certain to spend with God and slowly increase it. You will find that when you spend quality time with God, it makes you yearn to be with him even more.

When we come to know God, we begin realizing how much we need him and his loving presence in our lives. He becomes the friend, consoler, confidant, and Father who brings us the most peace and joy. He never leaves our side, and we can call upon him whenever we need a listening ear and compassionate heart. In a world that often confuses, criticizes, condemns, and frightens us, God, in contrast, consoles, heals, encourages, enlightens, liberates, and loves us. Suddenly, silence fills us with peace instead of boredom; the rosary compels us to be more like Jesus and Mary instead of putting us to sleep; and Mass becomes a time to hear God speak instead of a time to zone out. While it may be daunting to have a relationship with someone who isn't physically present, it is well worth the effort. In time, you will find that God *can* be seen, felt, and heard in our everyday lives.

The Fruits of True Prayer

You can recognize a life of true prayer by its fruits. When the two disciples finally realized they were talking to the risen Christ, they shared Jesus' message with others: "Then the two recounted what had taken place on the way" (Luke 24:35). The encounter radically changed them. They were no longer the two "downcast" disciples who fled the scene when their leader, Jesus, was condemned to die. Their sorrow had turned into joy, their hopelessness to faith, and their doubts to belief. More significantly, they had become passionate witnesses for Christ.

Likewise, our life of prayer and encounters with the risen Christ will create a radical change in us. How can we expect anything less? When we come face to face with Christ, he challenges us to see what he sees and to love how he loves. His light of perfection causes us to take a deep look within ourselves and note just how far we have gone astray. His purity and selflessness shine brightly against our unrighteousness and egotism. His great humility illuminates our stubborn pride, and his compassion, our mercilessness.

Our relationship with God draws us to action. Prayer extends outward. God inspires us to continue Christ's mission and fulfill our own roles as priest, prophet, and king. Just as the two disciples went out and proclaimed the Good News, so also are we called to bring people to God, speak his truth, and lead others to the greatness God has planned for everyone. These are the fruits that come from a life lived with God—a radical change within us and a faith that emboldens us to become the "hands and feet" of Jesus here on earth, as St. Teresa of Ávila so eloquently described it.

Our works of service (or lack thereof) are the most telling fruits of our prayer life because service and prayer are inextricably linked. The more we listen to the voice of God, the more we will hear his call to serve others. Make no mistake, our prayer lives are meaningless if we are not becoming more like Christ who came not to be served but to serve (see James 2:14–26). Our beloved saints had intimate relationships with

God, and through them, all were compelled to use their gifts to glorify God and care for his people, our brothers and sisters in Christ. They fed the hungry, comforted the afflicted, clothed the naked, buried the dead, and so much more. Jesus continually reminds his disciples that our love for God is shown by how well we love our neighbor: For "whatever you did for one of these least brothers of mine, you did for me" (Matthew 25:40).

The health of our prayer life and relationship with God can be examined by its fruits. Jesus said, "Every good tree bears good fruit, and a rotten tree bears bad fruit" (Matthew 7:17). When we allow God to reign in our heart and life, we bear good fruit by becoming increasingly more Christlike. When we keep him at arm's length, the fruit we produce will be limited and, depending on how far we push God aside, may even rot. Therefore, continually observe your prayer life and ask the Holy Spirit to help you draw nearer to God in thought, word, and action.

Let the Life-Changing Relationship Begin!

We are like those disciples on the road to Emmaus. God walks among us, but do we recognize him? I had the fortunate opportunity of encountering God at the most unlikely of places—the DMV. As I stood at the back of the line, the woman in front of me asked, "So what are you in for?"

"Renewing my license," I responded. "You?"

"I am here to renew a bus license," she said. "I take volunteers to visit convalescent homes."

"That's wonderful! What made you choose this population to serve?" I inquired.

"I was a drug addict for years and found myself homeless and severely underweight," she said. "Finally, enough was enough. One night, I gave myself over to God, stopped doing drugs, and this is when I felt called to give back. The elderly are often just dropped in homes, and their families hardly visit—if at all. They are so lonely, so I started this ministry."

I stared at her, awestruck. "How incredible it is that through God's grace you were able to stop doing drugs and, even more, that you chose to follow his call and serve those in need."

"Yes, it is" she replied, beaming. She reached for her wallet, grabbed a photo and showed it to me. It was a picture of her in her twenties. Long, disheveled hair obscured her face, and her emaciated body was hunched over a kitchen table. "This was me around that time. I keep it with me as a reminder of how far I have come."

I nodded and smiled back at her. "May I ask how you were able to escape homelessness?"

"That was another miracle God worked in my life," she said, eyes brightening. "I would go door to door asking people if I could wash their cars, pull their weeds, or do anything else to earn money. Some people would automatically slam the door and kick me out because of my appearance. Thankfully, there were some who appreciated that I was willing to work for them. Once I had earned enough, I decided to finish my degree and start a business in interior design."

"Wow, your life is truly inspiring," I replied with wide-eyed wonder.

She nodded and replied, "All thanks to God!"

We reached the front of the line, and as we parted ways, I smiled to myself as I realized how I experienced the road to Emmaus story firsthand. Truly, God was speaking to me through this woman. My encounter only strengthened my conviction that prayer has the power to pardon, heal, and transform. She is a living, modern-day resurrection story. She sought God's forgiveness and help, and God answered her in surprising ways. The more the woman continued to seek God in prayer, the more she was blessed, and the more good God was able to do through her. Her intimacy with God changed her entire life. What once was a life full of despair, bitterness, and bondage was transformed into a life full of hope, joy, and peace.

God wants to be part of your life, too. Like this incredible woman, he wants to work miracles through you. He waits for you and longs for you. He continually knocks on the doors of your heart. Will you answer his call? Will you let him enter and allow him to be a part of your life? The choice is yours. May your relationship with God grow stronger each day and may this conversation with God change your life in the most beautiful ways.

For Practice and Reflection

God desires to be with you in the here and now. Let the life-changing conversation begin through the following exercise:

A Walk with God

1. Take a stroll outside in a remote and quiet place.

2. Imagine Christ beside you as you walk. For example, picture his appearance, gait, posture, and facial expression.

3. What would you like to tell God right now? Mentally share it with him.

4. Reflect on all you have learned about God's love for you and visualize Jesus responding to what you just said. What is his demeanor like when you speak (for example: concerned, joyful, sad)? What does he do (for example: embrace you, place an arm around your shoulder)? What does he say?

5. Continue your walk and repeat steps three and four until you finish sharing everything that has been on your heart and mind this past week.

6. Find a peaceful, secluded spot to thank God for this time together.

LET THE LIFE-CHANGING CONVERSATION BEGIN!

〰
〰

The two disciples couldn't recognize Jesus because they were blinded by despair. What has blinded you from seeing God in your life? What has helped open your eyes to his presence?

"You can recognize a life of true prayer by its fruits," writes the author. How has God challenged you to make changes in your life? How has your prayer life borne fruit?

Can you think of someone who has been transformed through a life of prayer and God's grace? Describe his or her story.

Bibliography

"America's Changing Religious Landscape." Pewforum.org. Pew Research Center, May 12, 2015.

Ávila, Teresa. *The Collected Works of St. Teresa of Ávila,* Volume Two. Translated by Kieran Kavanaugh and Otilio Rodriguez, Institute of Carmelite Studies, 1980.

Dogmatic Constitution on Divine Revelation *(Dei Verbum).* Vatican.va. Second Vatican Council, 1965.

Jones, Jeffrey. "U.S. Church Membership Falls Below Majority for First Time." News.Gallup.com. Gallup, March 29, 2021.

Leonhardt, Douglas. *Finding God in All Things.* A Marquette Prayer Book. Marquette University, 2009.

Lipka, Michael. "Key Findings About American Catholics." Pewresearch.org. Pew Research Center, September 2, 2015.

Lisieux, Thérèse (of). *Story of a Soul: The Autobiography of St. Thérèse of Lisieux.* Translated by John Clarke, third edition. ICS Publications, 1996.

Lisieux, Thérèse (of). *St. Therese of Lisieux: Her Last Conversations.* Translated by John Clarke, first edition. ICS Publications, 1977.

Merton, Thomas. *Entering the Silence: Becoming a Monk and Writer. The Journals of Thomas Merton. Volume 2:1941–52.* Harper Collins, 1996.

Merton, Thomas. *Love and Living.* Mariner Books, 2002.

Merton, Thomas. *No Man Is an Island.* Harcourt Brace, 1955.

New American Bible, revised edition. Confraternity of Christian Doctrine, 2010.

Nouwen, Henri. *Discernment: Reading the Signs of Daily Life.* HarperOne, 2015.

"Religious Landscape Study." Pewforum.org. Pew Research Center, 2014.

Saad, Lydia. "Catholics' Church Attendance Resumes Downward Slide." News.Gallup.com. Gallup, April 9, 2018.

United States Catholic Conference, Inc. *English Translation of the Catechism of the Catholic Church for the United States of America* (1997). Trinity Communications, 2021.

CPSIA information can be obtained
at www.ICGtesting.com
Printed in the USA
FSHW021508121021

9 780764 828416